CELEBRATING DELHI

Edited by

MALA DAYAL

RAVI DAYAL Publisher

PENGUIN
VIKING

VIKING
Published by the Penguin Group
Penguin Books India Pvt. Ltd, 11 Community Centre, Panchsheel Park, New Delhi 110 017, India
Penguin Group (USA) Inc., 375 Hudson Street, New York, New York 10014, USA
Penguin Group (Canada), 90 Eglinton Avenue East, Suite 700, Toronto, Ontario, Canada M4P 2Y3 (a division of Pearson Penguin Canada Inc.)
Penguin Books Ltd, 80 Strand, London WC2R 0RL, England
Penguin Ireland, 25 St Stephen's Green, Dublin 2, Ireland (a division of Penguin Books Ltd)
Penguin Group (Australia), 250 Camberwell Road, Camberwell, Victoria 3124, Australia (a division of Pearson Australia Group Pty Ltd)
Penguin Group (NZ), 67 Apollo Drive, Rosedale, North Shore 0632, New Zealand (a division of Pearson New Zealand Ltd)
Penguin Group (South Africa) (Pty) Ltd, 24 Sturdee Avenue, Rosebank, Johannesburg 2196, South Africa

Penguin Books Ltd, Registered Offices: 80 Strand, London WC2R 0RL, England

First published in Viking by Penguin Books India and Ravi Dayal Publisher 2010

'A Kayastha's View of Delhi' by Ravi Dayal first appeared in *Seminar* 515.

10 9 8 7 6 5 4 3 2

ISBN 9780670084821

Typeset in Sabon by Mantra Virtual Services, New Delhi
Printed at Gopsons Papers Ltd, Noida

This anthology is dedicated to
Ravi Dayal 1937–2006
The quintessential Dilliwala, unapologetic 'bidi' smoker, uncompromising publisher and editor, loyal friend and relation, who helped structure this series of lectures on the city he loved, its refinement and its language 'as yet untainted by Punjabi'.

Contents

Introduction

This book is a compilation of eleven lectures held at the India International Centre (IIC) over a nine-month period in 2006. Originally titled the 'Sir Sobha Singh Memorial Lectures', they were organized by The Attic (Amarjit Bhagwant Singh Charitable Trust) in collaboration with the IIC and INTACH (Indian National Trust for Art and Cultural Heritage). In their subject matter, planning and inspiration they owed everything to informal and insightful discussions with Naina Dayal and Ravi Dayal, to whom the lecture series and now this book is dedicated.

Sobha Singh was a twenty-two-year-old contractor working on the Kalka–Simla railroad when he visited Delhi in 1911. He was present at the Delhi Darbar at which King George V declared that the capital of British India would be shifted from Calcutta to Delhi. He saw his opportunity and took it.

'Rarely was a man so identified with the birth of a city as Sir Sobha Singh was with New Delhi, translating into sandstone and marble most of the imperial blueprints of Lutyens and Baker. Few builders in the world have left behind as tributes to their genius such an imposing list of edifices encompassing most of the colonial face of Delhi as he has done,' says Khushwant Singh.

The original introduction to the series of lectures is as good an introduction to the book as it was to the lectures: 'This series of lectures encompasses many facets of the life of Delhi—its history, architecture, cuisine, music, environment, and the arts.'

The first lecture (and article) 'My Father the Builder' by Khushwant Singh, author, historian and raconteur, set the tone and style for the series. His celebrity status ensured a huge audience with more people who couldn't get in to hear him than those who did. At the age of ninety, his memory was undimmed, his style elegant, his scholarship undoubted and his humour undiminished. This is a first-hand account of the building of New Delhi and the important role his father Sir Sobha Singh played in its construction. He talks of the building of this imperial city which he witnessed 'rising in front of my eyes' set against the backdrop of the personalities, English and Indian, who made it possible.

Most of us see Delhi as a city of imposing medieval forts, palaces and tombs. But Upinder Singh in 'Discovering the Ancient in Modern Delhi' strongly believes that the less 'sexy' ancient remains, the broken bits of pottery, the prehistoric stone tools, the glazed earthenware and the stone pillars tell an equally fascinating story. She suggests that the antiquity of the Purana Qila could go back to 1000 BC and may even be linked to the legendary city of Indraprastha mentioned in the Mahabharata. Excavations in the villages of Anangpur, Kharkhari Nahar, Bhorgarh and Mandoli of the National Capital Region of Delhi have revealed that they were stone age and Harappan sites. She says that with a cultivated sensibility ordinary ancient remains can be animated by imagination.

Place names are where 'history and geography intersect' and Narayani Gupta in her piece 'Delhi's History as Reflected in Its Toponymy' uses place names to unearth a vanishing history of Delhi. The 'kots' and 'sarais', the 'purs' and 'paharis' contain the true romance of Delhi's past. Firoze Shah Kotla, Sarai Kale Khan, Badarpur, and Paharganj are just a few of the names that have survived the onslaught of our new political classes. 'Place-names have a meaning in the language and in local history and are part of the cultural fabric of the city. At every point,' she says, 'when we name or rename places we lose a little bit of history and risk becoming a city of Nehru Nagars and Veer Savarkar Margs.'

The thirteenth century saw the beginning of a brilliant era of Sufi Islam in India that continues to this day. In his article 'The Pir's Barakat and the Servitor's Ardour: the contrasting history of two Sufi shrines in Delhi', Sunil Kumar notes that in spite of its magnificent forts, mosques and tombs the 'epithet for the city most frequently encountered in medieval sources—*Hazrat-i Dehli* or the auspicious, sacred city—is derived from the mystics, theologians, litterateurs and jurists who made this city their place of residence'. The Sufi mystics he notes are remembered not by the grandeur of their tombs but the simplicity of their graves and the intense spiritual emotion they evoked. The final resting place of a Sufi spiritual master provides the believer guidance and succour, his grace imbues the premises turning his grave into a place of pilgrimage. He compares the evolving histories of two small shrines: the flourishing sixteenth century one of Khwaja Maqbul Shah in Saket that has been lost to doctrinal Islam and the twentieth century anonymous grave that is now the flourishing shrine of Sayyid Jalal-uddin Chishti in the Jahanpanah forest.

Magnificent palaces, imposing forts and striking buildings are not built by kings and governments but by masons and stonecutters, bricklayers and loaders—people we choose not to see or care about. This vast army of the underprivileged, which includes the clerks, the drivers, the nurses are pushed to the periphery of the city and are regarded as a burden. Without basic civic amenities, the perpetual threat of 'illegality' and 'demolition' hangs over them in the name of a clean environment and tourism. Dunu Roy in his hard hitting article 'City Makers and City Breakers' asks who the real makers of a city are and confronts us with the reality of the refugee and resettlement colonies, the thousands of illegal slum dwellers and the blindness of the civic planners who refuse to acknowledge their presence.

In Mughal times the mango, sheesham and banyan were the favoured avenue trees but when choosing the trees that should line the avenues of Imperial New Delhi the British chose 'not a single species of tree that can be called a Delhi native'. Delving into archival records Pradip Krishen in 'Avenue Trees in Lutyens' Delhi: How They Were Chosen' finds that the choice of trees was a 'fundamental ecological miscalculation'. In their desire to avoid 'deciduousness' and 'commonness' the mango, sheesham and neem were ignored and some not excellent aesthetic and value judgements made about the trees to be planted.

Delhi has been for centuries the centre of political power and many great artists, poets and musicians have found patronage at its courts. Delhi has thus been home to a rich tradition of classical music. The 'Khalifa' of the 'Dilli Gharana' traces the roots of this style to the end of the thirteenth century when two different strands of music developed—music inspired by the Sufi traditions of Central Asia and the 'darbari' (courtly) style. The Sufi style developed into what is now 'qawwali', while the 'darbari' continued in the classical dhrupad dhamar style. Many centuries later, these two styles fused to form a composite now known as the Delhi Gharana. This style, says Vidya Rao in 'The Dilli Gharana', has a distinct identity. It is an extraordinary mix of dhrupad-dhamar, khayal, tarana and also draws from folk music forms like jhoola, geet, qaul and dhamar.

On the evening of Tuesday, 6 February 2007, we were treated to a wonderful performance of the Delhi Gharana by Ustad Iqbal Khan, the Khalifa of this style, preceded by Vidya Rao's talk.

No account of the history of Delhi can be complete without a detailed examination of the 'mutiny' or the 'war of independence' of 1857. Using recently translated archival material and writing this history from an Indian perspective, William Dalrymple in his book *The Last Mughal: The Eclipse of a Dynasty* captures the last days of the dazzling Mughal capital and its final destruction in the uprising. One of the surprising elements in this history is the use of 'Religious Rhetoric in the Delhi Uprising of 1857'. In an era remarkably similar to ours in this respect, the Mujahideen were fighting a 'jihad' to rid the country of 'kafirs', Hindu sepoys were fighting for their 'dharma' and the British chaplain John Midgley Jennings was exhorting the faithful to 'be preparing to conquer the subcontinent for Anglicanism and the one true God'. As we know Anglicanism triumphed but with a savagery and barbarity reminiscent of the Mongol chieftain Taimur and the Persian King, Nadir Shah.

We were not able to include pieces by all the speakers of the Delhi series in this book, either because they did not send their articles or due to the constraints of this book. An excellent talk by Sheila Chhabra, 'Dilli ke totay, mainay aur thoray bahar ke mehman—Common birds of Delhi and some interesting winter visitors', could not be included without the beautiful colour slides that accompanied the talk, nor could we include 'Dehli ki Aakhri Shama', a poetic re-enactment of the *Last Mush'aira of Delhi* directed by Rakhshanda Jalil and enacted by the faculty and students of Jamia Millia Islamia. We have however added three articles that were not part of the original series. These articles are on the food, the language and a personal view of Delhi soon after Independence.

'Dilli ka Asli Khana' (The Real Cuisine of Delhi) by Priti Narain is a fascinating glimpse not only into the foods of Delhi but the history and culture that produced it. Buddhists, Jains, Central Asians, the Sultans and the Mughals followed each other over the centuries each producing and introducing dishes and ingredients—everything from simple vegetables without onions as they 'caused pain, ruined the eyesight and weakened the body', to rose-flavoured sherbets, meat-filled samosas, Samarkand apples, Portuguese pineapples, elaborate biryanis and the mouth-watering foods that make the North Indian and Delhi cuisines among the best in the world.

Tokyo has Japanese, Moscow has Russian, London has English and Delhi is polyglot. There seems not to have ever been a common language for Delhi. When the rulers spoke Turkic or Persian or Urdu or English the masses spoke Braj or Dehlavi or Punjabi or Hindustani and this rich Creole forms the texture of the linguistic expression of the city. Rarely has a city been occupied and 're-culturized' as often as Delhi by invading armies, foreign kings, nomadic adventurers, wandering Sufis and assorted colonialists in search of spices or trade routes or conversions. Each group brought amongst other things its language adding yet another layer to this city of Babel but also taking away. Sohail Hashmi in 'The Language of Delhi' shows how words like the Persian 'sepah' and the Urdu 'sipahi' became the colonial 'sepoy' and how idea, style, house, hospital, bisicle (bicycle), pension, file, office, car are now Hindustani words.

The last piece included in the book 'A Kayastha's View of Delhi' by Ravi Dayal, the quintessential 'dilliwalla', is a very personal account of post-Independence Delhi. With his trademark humour and a heavy dose of nostalgia he writes about the Mathur Kayasthas of Delhi. The Kayastha community, scribes to the Mughals, considered themselves dilliwallas *par excellence* and the ultimate in refinement, not least because they were 'speakers of a tongue untainted by Punjabi'. He remembers the culinary delights of 'shahar' (Shahjahanabad), 'the classical view of the dhobis washing and drying clothes on the river bank' and tongas piled high with tin trunks, holdalls and baskets, clattering down the well trodden streets of a now vanished age.

Mala Dayal, the editor of the book, has worked patiently and closely with the authors. She has suggested many of the additions, especially the article on cooking to make this book as complete and interesting as possible and reflecting the many unique facets of the life of Delhi that make it both a frustrating and a rewarding city to live in.

Preminder Singh

Khushwant Singh

My Father the Builder

I start with an apology. I have done no research on the building of New Delhi. My knowledge is largely derived from what I've read about Lutyens and his colleague Herbert Baker and what I heard from my father. But by the time he got talking to me he had begun to romanticize his past and the buildings he had made. I don't know how reliable his information was. What I am going to say is largely based on what I saw myself. When I was brought to Delhi at the age of three or four from my village, there was no New Delhi. Now, having lived here most of the ninety-three years of my life, I can't find my way about the city.

I had better start by telling you of my family background. The village from where we came was called Hadali. It was a small hamlet a few miles west of the river Jhelum and a few miles south of the Khewra Salt Range from which rock salt is hewn to this day. My recollection is that it looked rather like the Sahara desert, or parts of Rajasthan. It had sand dunes, a few date palm trees. Over 95 per cent of the population was Muslims of Baluch extraction—Waddhals, Janjuas, Mastials, Awans, Noons and Tiwanas. Our relations were cordial. Every elder person was a chacha, every elder woman was a maasi. The main occupation of the Muslims was soldiering. Just about every young man enlisted for the army. They didn't have any education, so none of them ever became officers. But they were strapping, tall, handsome men. Many of them made it to the Viceroy's bodyguard. Even after we moved to Delhi those relationships continued. Their womenfolk came to call on my grandmother and mother, the men called on my father.

I can only trace my ancestors back to a few generations. My father Sobha Singh had a younger brother Ujjal Singh, who later became minister then governor of Punjab and Tamil Nadu. Their father Sujan Singh, after whom many buildings are named, was the real founder of the fortunes of this family. He named many factories that he built after his father Inder Singh: in Mian Channu, Jaranwala, and Sargodha. Inder Singh's father was Pyare Lal. It was he who converted to the Khalsa form of Sikhism. We were Khuranas by caste. Our home in Hadali was a large haveli. In the deorhi there was a colour print of Guru Nanak on one wall and facing it a picture of Mallika Queen Victoria. The usual practice after the *rehras* evening prayer was to turn to both pictures in turn, bow and recite: *Raja raj karey, praja sukhi rahey* (May the Sovereign rule and his subjects be happy). The tradition of loyalty to the British came down three generations.

Our business at that time was taking camel caravans with rock salt from the Khewra mines to Lahore, Amritsar and Punjab's other cities and in exchange bringing oil, spices, tea, sugar and textiles to sell in the villages around Hadali. It was reasonably profitable. We were the most prosperous family of our village. Later the family started acquiring land and we spread our business operations to places like Sargodha and Jaranwala, putting up cotton ginning and spinning factories and growing cotton or indigo to supply to the British mills in Lancashire. This continued till we shifted to Delhi.

Now to Delhi. The story starts on 12 December 1911, when King George V and Queen Mary came to Delhi for the Coronation Durbar. Amongst the many things they said and did was to announce the shifting of the capital from Calcutta to Delhi. It was a well-guarded secret—no one knew about it till this announcement was made. To put the seal on their decision they planted two foundation stones, one by the King, the other by the Queen, in what came to be known as Kingsway. There was opposition by the European business community of Calcutta. Both Lord Curzon and Mahatma Gandhi opposed the move. The Viceroy, Lord Hardinge, dismissed all objections and decided to go ahead. The following year, that is 1912, Captain Swinton of the London County Council to which the job had been entrusted, consulted the Royal British Institute of Architects to suggest the name of an architect. They recommended the name of Edwin Landseer Lutyens. In turn, Lutyens suggested the name of Herbert Baker with whom he had worked earlier in South Africa. In 1912, Swinton and the two architects arrived in Delhi. They had a look at the place where the King and Queen had planted foundation stones and decided it was an unsuitable site for the new city. They scouted around Delhi on elephants and horseback, looking for a suitable site and ultimately came to the conclusion that the better place was village Malcha on Raisina Hill. It was on an elevation and had the ridge behind from which they could quarry stone.

Lutyens and Baker were sent round the country to see works of great Indian architecture. Both the King and the Viceroy were of the opinion that the new city should be in the traditional Indian style. They saw Hindu temples, Buddhist stupas, the Taj Mahal, palaces in Bikaner, and Mandu. They came back convinced that there was no such thing as an 'Indian tradition of architecture'. They put it in writing, 'They are just mushroom dynasties who built big buildings.' This is true. Our forefathers knew how to build forts as good as any in the world, they knew how to build palaces where royal families could live in grand style, they knew how to build mausoleums where they were buried and places of worship like mosques and temples but they did not build things like large panchayat houses, a parliament house or legislative assembly buildings. They did not build courts of justice nor civil servants' offices or quarters. These were alien concepts.

They built durbar halls like the 'diwan-e-aam' or 'diwan-e-khas' but nothing of use for commoners. The Viceroy and the King were upset with the report submitted by Lutyens and Baker. A compromise was arrived at: the architects agreed to give their buildings external semblances of Indianness. The three items they chose were a sun breaker (chajja), a latticed window (jali), and the dome (gumbad) which they called the *chattri* (umbrella). So you have these external embellishments that resemble Oriental architecture. The rest is almost entirely British. They said that the concept of law and order that the British brought to India should be exhibited in the style of the buildings that they were making. Their opinion was accepted. There were still lingering doubts over the choice of Raisina Hill as the best site. There is a lovely account written by Baker of how the final decision was made. During the monsoons, he and some of his friends rode up to Raisina Hill. They were standing on top. It was raining intermittently. As he looked down at the vast collection of ruins of cities, tombs and monuments lying below them—a scene of total desolation—he was filled with doubts about his decision. Suddenly the rain stopped, the clouds cleared and a huge rainbow spanned the horizon ending where India Gate stands today. This was a good omen.

The first job my father then about eighteen years old got was to transplant the two foundation stones from Kingsway to Raisina Hill. It had to be done in the stealth of the night lest superstitious Indians construe it an ill omen. He hired a bullock-cart, packed the stones in it and rode on his bicycle alongside through the city suburbs in the light of petromax lamps, and implanted the two stones of what was to become the capital of India. He did not tell me what he was paid for it.

World War I (1914–18) broke out. Everything was suspended for the duration of the War. Work was taken up after 1919. Lutyens was forty-two when he returned. A line that you should bear in mind was what he inscribed on a casket he presented to his fiancée Emily when they got engaged.

She was Lord Lytton's daughter, which in no small way helped him to get the job of planning New Delhi. The line read: 'As faith wills, faith fulfills'—if you have the self-confidence to do something, things will turn your way and you will be able to achieve your aims. He began to put his plans on paper. He wanted to make an amphitheatre on the ridge and use the stone to build the main structures such as the Viceregal Lodge and the two Secretariats. He found that the stone from the ridge was unsuitable. So both he and Baker decided to use the stone used by the Mughals which had to be brought from the Vindhyachal mountains and other places in central India; marble from Makrana and Jaipur; and both stone and marble from Dholpur. Earlier calculations of costs went awry. Lutyens' major plan was to dam the Yamuna, behind Humayun's tomb, create a huge lake and make a riverside boulevard around it. He also wanted Kingsway (today's Rajpath) going straight from the Viceregal Lodge through India Gate up to the southern entrance of the Purana Qila which is no longer used. Also, another road leading from the South Block to the southern entrance of the Jama Masjid. The cost was astronomical. So the plan of damming the river and creating a riverside boulevard had to be abandoned. The idea of a road leading to the Jama Masjid had also to be abandoned because it ran through Gurdwara Rakabganj and the Sikhs were up in arms. The cost of breaking through the Mughal wall and buying whole bazaars would be exorbitant. Lord Hardinge became somewhat peevish. An attempt was made on his life while he was riding in procession in Chandni Chowk. Terrorists threw a bomb which killed his umbrella bearer and almost killed him. He kept turning down Lutyens' plans as too expensive. Lutyens wrote in a terse note, 'The Viceroy thinks only of the next three years, I am thinking of the next 300 years.' You can see the man's vision of the future. If we didn't have Rajpath where would our Republic Day parades take place? He sensed that in course of time India would become independent and would be ruled by the Indians themselves. However, he had to make compromises here and there. Then he had disagreements with Baker, which became public knowledge. He wanted the Viceregal Lodge designed by him to be on a higher level than the Secretariats designed by Baker. He thought the head of state should be put at a higher elevation than his civil servants. Baker believed that in the prevailing air of democracy the ruler and his civil servants should be on the same level. The Viceroy and the King approved of Baker's idea. The bigger quarrel was over the gradient. As you come down the road from Rashtrapati Bhavan between the two Secretariats you will notice a gentle slope. Lutyens wanted it to be at a steeper angle so that the Viceregal Lodge could be seen from a distance, from the base to the top. Baker held that a gentle incline would look better and it didn't matter whether or not you could see the Viceregal Lodge from the base to the top. Again, Baker won and Lutyens was overruled. The two architects stopped talking to each other. Nevertheless, the new city proceeded to be built.

My memory goes back to the time when there was no city but a lot of brick kilns. There was a miniature train, which ran from Badarpur up to what is now Connaught Circus. It was called the Imperial Delhi Railway. It was a narrow-gauge railway line that brought sand, gravel, stones and other building material and deposited them at different sites. The contractors got the labour, largely Bagaris, from Rajasthan. At one time there were 30,000 of them in Delhi. There were also Bandhanis from Punjab who were tougher and bigger so they could carry the heavier loads and there were Sangtarash (masons) descendants of the people who built the Taj. They worked under the instructions of a master mason, a Scotsman named Cairn. Contractors lived along what was then called Old Mill Road, because of a wheat grinding *chakkee*. It ran along the circle outside Parliament House, where a small mosque and the late President Fakhruddin Ali Ahmed's grave is situated. My grandparents, parents and my elder brother and I lived in a large shack. My earliest recollection is of being woken up by the deafening roar of the 'ara' machines cutting stones with iron saws into different sizes, and the tick, tick, tick of masons chiselling stones into patterns designed by Cairns. This went on all day till late in the evening. When the work stopped and the ara machines fell silent we witnessed an unforgettable spectacle. Bagaris, who were paid eight annas a day for a man and six annas for a woman, lived in jhomparis, ate unleavened, coarse bread with chillies or salt, would return to their huts singing lustily, their women's ghararas swinging as if without a care in the world, while our families who made money were quarrelling over '*bahi khaataa kitna hua kam, kitna nahi hua*' and that kind of thing. Soon the builders became prosperous. It didn't take them very long to make money on the side. They used the surplus stocks of cement, stones and bricks to build themselves big houses on what is today Jantar Mantar Road extending from Ashoka Road at one end to Parliament Street (Sansad Marg) with the Free Church and the Planetarium at the other. I spent all my school and college years in the one my father built and named 'Baikunth' (paradise). It is today Kerala House. Our next-door neighbour was Baisakha Singh, my father's closest friend. They breached the dividing wall so that they could go across without having to come in through the front gates. The house next to Baisakha Singh's was an enormous mansion of stone and marble built by Dharam Singh Sethi, who at one time was the richest of the contractors as he had the monopoly of supplying marble, granite and sandstone from quarries in Dholpur. Next to him was Ram Singh Kabli. Facing us was Rai Bahadur Narain Singh from Sangrur. He had been a peasant, and rumoured to have belonged to a gang of dacoits. He got his share of the contracting business. His son Ranjit Singh, however, made more money out of his sugar mills in Uttar Pradesh and the Imperial Hotel on Janpath that is still owned by his descendants. They were known as the 'panj pyaras', the first five disciples of the last Sikh Guru Gobind Singh. There were other contractors notably Akbar Ali of Jhelum and Seth Haroon from Sind, who were Muslims.

Slowly the city began to rise. By 1922, building materials

were in place. Contracts were going-a-begging. My father bagged the South Block of the Secretariat; Baisakha Singh the North Block. The Viceregal Lodge as well as Vijay Chowk were shared by many, as were roads, houses for senior officials and quarters for clerks. By 1923 or 1924, the new city began to take shape. You couldn't believe that in what had been a wilderness a metropolis was beginning to rise. Lutyens looked into every detail. As soon as he marked out the roads, trees were planted on either side. Pradip Krishen will tell you who chose the trees and their suitability.

New Delhi was meant to take about four to five years to build; it actually took nearly sixteen. But by 1929 the major buildings had been completed. Our rulers decided that an inauguration was in order. Lord Irwin was the Viceroy. Before I come to the inauguration let me tell you of one incident that has never left my mind. Among the many buildings my father made was the War Memorial Arch, today's India Gate. This incident took place during the last stages when they were finishing the top part. There was a huge crane which took up the workmen with bricks, mortar or cement right to the top, dropped them there and then brought them back. It had a squarish wooden platform and four steel chains to hold on to. One day a woman labourer working on top wanted to come down. She got on to the platform as it landed. It moved aside into space; she slipped and fell to her death. The husband had to be paid between two to four hundred rupees to buy another wife.

By 1929, the major buildings had been completed. Captain Swinton of the London County Council, who had come there when there was nothing there but wilderness, came to see what had been put up. He recorded: 'There has risen before us all to see, in all its majestic glory the Viceroy's House. One looks, one accepts and one marvels.' Not everyone shared his enthusiasm. Beverly Nichols described it as 'a British matron in fancy dress' because of the jalis, chajjas and chattris.

Among other monuments my father built was the slender

Jaipur Column in front of the Viceregal Lodge. What is notable is the inscription which echoed Lutyens' sentiments. When the Viceroy asked Lutyens to suggest words to be inscribed, he replied frivolously, 'No dogs should be allowed to go on the ramp.' In a more serious mood, he suggested the following, 'Endow your thought with faith, your deed with courage, your life with sacrifice. So all men may know the greatness of India.' Irwin shortened it to, 'In thought faith, in word wisdom, in deed courage, in life sacrifice, so may India be great.'

I come to the last part: the personal reminiscences of my grandfather Sujan Singh who showed the way to prosperity to his two sons. I have faint recollections of him. He was a powerfully built man with a flowing white beard covering his chest. Although prosperous, he used to haggle with vegetable-sellers for paltry sums of money in annas and paisas till he brought them down. He was a stickler for saving money. He often told his sons, '*Aj ik rupayya bunk vich pao, sau saal baad, sood-dar-sood, ik lakh ban vaisee.*' (You put one rupee in a bank today, in a hundred years it will collect compound interest and become one lakh.) He was also very conservative and ill-tempered.

My father, Sobha Singh, was way ahead of his times. My elder brother Bhagwant and I were enrolled in Modern School which had just opened in Daryaganj. It was the first co-educational institution in Delhi. Amongst other things they taught us carpentry, gardening and music—how to play the dilruba or esraj. At one annual Foundation Day, my father took his father Sujan Singh with him. My grandfather discovered that some teachers were women. He saw us playing the esraj. He was furious. He came home and went for my father, '*Putraan noo miraasi bananae*?' (You want your sons to become street singers?) Thereafter he referred to us as *runn mureed* (disciples of lowly women). His special term of affection for me was *bharua* (pimp). I was there when he died at Mian Channu, surrounded by his wife, sons, daughters-in-law and grandchildren. Though owner of a sizeable fortune in land, factories and real estate (a railway station between Mian Channu and Khanewal still bears his name, Kot Sujan Singh) what worried him most was that he was leaving an uncleared debt of one lakh rupees to his sons. For him, owing money to anyone was a cardinal sin.

My father, Sobha Singh, was a very different kind of person. As I said earlier he was way ahead of his times. He sensed that if he had to get on with the English, he must know their language. He advertised for a tutor. A man called Desai from Poona came and stayed with us for some years. After the day's work, my father sat for a couple of hours poring over English texts with his Maharashtrian tutor. Within three or four years, he was able to speak the language fluently. He tried to get my mother to pick up English too. He hired an Anglo-Indian lady, Mrs Wright, to teach her. After months of slogging at it, my mother picked up a few words: good morning, good evening, good night and thank you. And she used to make fun of herself and converted the thank you to 'thankus very muchus'. Trying to train her how to mix with the English was a near disaster. She was vegetarian, like all the women in our families were. My father would take her to dinner parties given by his English friends. The only thing she could eat was asparagus, for which she developed a passion. Every time the bearer came with the second course—she couldn't eat the soup—she would off-load the entire asparagus dish meant for twelve people onto her plate. My father would hiss at her, '*Kuchh horan vaste vee chad de*' (Leave something for the others) and she would hiss back, '*Te main bhukki maran? Main hor kujh ni kha sakni*' (You want me to die of hunger? I can't eat anything else). He gave up the battle to Anglicize her.

My father was a six-footer and slimly built. My mother barely five feet tall. He was very particular about his attire. He wore English suits: coat and striped trousers, bow tie or silk ties and dinner jackets. I never saw him in shervanis and chooridars. The only Indian thing he wore was a *tehmat* when he retired for the night. He loved to eat and drink well: a huge breakfast of cornflakes, eggs, toast and fruit; a couple of gins and tonic before lunch which was also substantial; tea included cakes or pastry; he liked a couple of Scotches before dinner which was again an elaborate multiple-dish affair followed by a cognac or two. He never put on weight. He slept soundly both in the afternoons and at night. Sound sleep was the secret of his longevity.

He was reckless in his hospitality. There was never a time when he did not have guests staying with him in 'Baikunth' in Delhi or his large house 'Sunderban' in Mashobra, six miles from Simla. Many stayed for months on end. Among regular visitors to his house were Rajagopalachari, Mohammed Ali Jinnah, Sir Tej Bahadur Sapru and Mr Jayakar. When I was in Delhi, I often saw Mahatma Gandhi strolling in my father's garden talking to Mr Jinnah. Even during World War II my father never missed having parties. Once he got the list of guests staying at Gables Hotel in Mashobra and invited all the Europeans, Englishmen on leave, their wives and women whose husbands were serving at the front. There must have been over fifty of them. He arranged for a Goan band to play dance music. The invitees introduced themselves, drank, ate and danced. Sunderban had a wooden dance floor, a grand piano and a full-sized billiards table with a room of its own. Sometime later, I asked him what he got out of his reckless hospitality. He told me that soon after his bash in Mashobra he was returning to Delhi and found himself seated next to an Englishman in uniform in the rail car going to Kalka. The man introduced himself as one of his guests at Sunderban. They got talking. My father landed a lucrative contract to supply provisions to the army.

It was odd that he was as eager to get rid of his guests as he was on inviting them over, something that I have inherited from him. Hardly had his invitees finished their post-dinner coffees and liqueurs, he would start fidgeting. The slightest move on the part of any of his guests and he would ask, '*Motor mangavan?*' (Shall I send for your car?) Everyone got the hint and departed. He kept that routine all his life.

My father's great passion was gardening. He grew the best grapefruit in the city and beds of strawberries that nobody could match. His garden had a great variety of exotic roses which he invited everyone to admire.

More important than being able to speak English fluently and the ability to mix with English people, was his foresight. It was remarkable that at a time when New Delhi was a barren waste, at an open auction he bought land in what is now Karol Bagh for two annas (tweve-and-a-half paise) a square yard. He later gifted this land to his clerical staff. In what is now Connaught Circus—probably the most expensive real estate in India, he bought land at two rupees a square yard—freehold. He was the first one to put up buildings there. The first was where the Wengers Block is now. If you look up above Wengers, there is a red sandstone slab that reads 'Sujan Singh Block', named after his father. It was first a general store run by a Parsi family called Framji's who sold cigars and chocolates and liquor. Framji couldn't make enough money from his venture and my father rented it to Wengers. He was the first man to build a cinema—the Regal—in the new city. The Regal building included a restaurant called Standard which later became Gaylord. He then built another cinema called Rivoli. At first, he tried to run it himself. I remember there were times when there were only ten people in the cinema and he had to beg them to take their money back and let him not waste money on showing a film. He was once approached by Uday Shankar, the dancer. Uday Shankar had just come back from his tour in Europe and got great write-ups. He wanted to rent Regal Cinema for a couple of nights. My father asked him, 'What for?' He said, 'I want to dance.' My father's idea of men dancing was only of hijras going round clapping their hands. Uday Shankar paid the money in advance, so my father agreed. Out of curiosity he went there to see who was going to see this man dance. He saw whole lines of cars of English people in their dinner jackets and their ladies going into the hall. So he also went in to see and realized that there was more to Indian dancing than hijras gyrating. He invited Uday Shankar and his troupe to his house to meet some of his English friends.

My father was a modest man. He did not name a single building after himself. The many he built and owned were named after his father, including Sujan Singh Park. One he named after his nephew Narinder, who he brought up as his son. Not one after his children. He built more of New Delhi than any other contractor. Besides the buildings mentioned earlier, he built the Chelmsford Club, AIFACS Hall, Broadcasting House (All India Radio), the National Museum, Dayal Singh College, TB Hospital, the Red Cross Building and Baroda House. And much else besides. He was the largest owner of private property in the city. People spoke of him as '*Aadhee nai dilli ka maalik*' (owner of half of New Delhi). Whatever recognition he got was from the British. He was knighted, he became a Member of the Council of States, and the first President of the New Delhi Municipal Committee. He had ambitions of getting into politics. He had Mr Jinnah come over from Bombay to attend my wedding to Kaval Malik, daughter of Sir Teja Singh Malik, the first Indian Chief Engineer of the CPWD. Their names appear in alcoves on either side in the South and North Blocks of the Secretariat. The slab on the South Block has his name on top followed by Dharam Singh, Baisakha Singh and four or five others. On the other side are names of architects and engineers: Lutyens, Baker and Teja Singh Malik. But not one road in this city is named after any one of them. You have doctors, lawyers and needless to say unknown, nondescript politicians after whom roads and parks have been named. Not one after the men who built New Delhi, neither Lutyens nor Baker, nor my father, nor Teja Singh Malik.

The last thing my father did was to create a charitable trust. He left all his children well provided for for generations to come. The rest of the property he had, that is Sujan Singh Park, the Ambassador Hotel, the big house in which he lived—Number 1 Janpath which is now rented out to the Hungarian

Cultural Centre—all that he left to a charitable trust outlining what he wished to be done. His preference was for a dharamshala, near a hospital, where relations of people being treated could come and stay. So we built one, in the SGTB hospital in Shahadra. We built a block for the Pingalwala in Amritsar. We built a block for the Tamanna School for mentally handicapped children. We built a clinic in Guwahati and gave money here and there and now we have committed ourselves to building a clinic-cum-night-shelter near Lahori Gate.

As I have mentioned before, despite his dietary indulgences my father kept in reasonably good health till he was in his eighties. His health began to deteriorate when he was about eighty-five. Nothing serious but generally declining. He became hard of hearing and slow in his movements. He remained fairly agile but became slower. But he continued to enjoy his evening drink. One evening when I was living in Bombay, he rang up my wife who was the only daughter-in-law who drank in his presence. He said, '*Main akkalah baitha han, tu aaja.*' (I am alone. Come over.) My mother and sister had gone shopping. My wife went over to join him for his evening drink. While they were exchanging gossip, my mother and sister returned. My father gave my wife permission to go back to her home. A few minutes later, she was rung up by my sister who told her that her father was not feeling well and asked her to come immediately. Before leaving, my wife rang me up in Bombay and told me, 'I'm going back to your father's, he is not feeling well.' By the time she got there, he was dead. He had just had his glass of whisky and complained he was not feeling well and lay down. And rose no more. As they say, he took one for the long road leading to the Unknown. The only tribute I could pay him later was in the words of Allama Iqbal which are in Persian. '*Nishaan e mard e momin ba goyam?*' (You ask me for the signs of a man of faith?) '*Choon marg aayad, tabassum bar lab-e-ost.*' (When death comes to him he has a smile on his lips.) What could be better than holding a glass of whisky in your hand when going to meet your Maker?

Upinder Singh

Discovering the Ancient in Modern Delhi

Over my many years as a teacher in St. Stephen's College, I often asked my students whether they could name any ancient remains in Delhi. There was usually a long silence, and then someone would mention the iron pillar in Mehrauli. When asked who was responsible for installing that pillar, the response usually was: 'Ashoka'. Now that iron pillar *is* ancient, but it was *not* set up by Ashoka.

This little anecdote leads me to a question: Why is the general level of awareness of Delhi's ancient past so dismal compared to the awareness of its medieval and modern history? I think part of the answer lies in the fact that the volume of available information is much lower for ancient times. An ancient history of the Delhi area can certainly be written on the basis of textual references, but it would be a very short and scrappy history as textual references are few. The archaeological evidence is a little more substantial. There are some reports of field surveys and excavations. Unfortunately, the full report of the large-scale excavations carried out between the 1950s and 1970s at the Purana Qila—a very important site—have still not been published. Apart from the volume of evidence, there is the issue of its visibility and its nature. Most books on Delhi's history are obsessed with the idea of its seven cities. This leaves little room for talking about the many pre-urban and non-urban settlements that existed in this area long, long ago.

Delhi's ancient remains have too much competition. Take the case of the Purana Qila. The visitor can hardly be blamed for carrying away memories of the beautiful medieval mosque built by Sher Shah and the intriguing octagonal structure on whose steps Humayun may have taken a fatal tumble. And it is perfectly understandable that most are left unmoved by the nondescript depression which marks the place where many exciting remains were discovered decades ago.

It is not really all that surprising that when it comes to Delhi's historical remains, most people think of magnificent medieval palaces, tombs and mosques or the imposing structures of the colonial period that dot the cityscape. These command the sort of attention that ancient remains such as humble stone tools, terracottas, and broken pieces of pottery simply do not. What makes it worse is that most of these ancient remains cannot be seen in their original setting, in fact most of them cannot be viewed at all. If you want to get acquainted with them, you will have to see them in museum displays or in illustrations in academic journals.

Can the scrappy, dislocated (and often invisible) leftovers of the lives of ordinary people who lived in ancient times compete for attention with the impressive medieval and modern structures built at the behest of powerful elites? The ability to appreciate them certainly requires a certain kind of sensibility. Some people have it, others don't, but it can be acquired. This is a sensibility that allows us to marvel at ordinary ancient things and to animate them by using the imagination.

The next few pages give a sample of some of the many exciting ancient remains discovered in the National Capital Region. I will then focus on a phenomenon that continues to fascinate me—the lives, adventures and misadventures of ancient remains in medieval and modern times, and the many different layers of meaning that they end up acquiring.

The oldest remains of human activity in the Delhi area

are prehistoric stone tools. The first such tools to be identified were four lower palaeolithic hand-axes, found in 1956 on the northern ridge, not far from the main gate of Delhi University. Many years later, B.M. Pande found a late Acheulian hand-axe on the campus of Jawaharlal Nehru University. If I correctly recall what Mr Pande told me many years ago, he had taken a bus to JNU to visit his friend B.D. Chattopadhyaya who used to teach there. He saw the hand-axe on the ground in front of him as he got off at the bus-stop. That's how major discoveries are often made! In 1985–86, Dilip Chakrabarti and Nayanjot Lahiri searched systematically for stone tools in south Delhi and the adjoining parts of Haryana. They found forty-three sites ranging from the lower palaeolithic (the earliest part of the Stone Age) to the microlithic (microliths are tiny stone tools that are especially associated with the mesolithic stage of prehistory).

The only prehistoric site in the Delhi area that has been excavated by archaeologists is at Anangpur, a picturesque village nestling in the Badarpur hills. Anangpur was already known for its Rajput–period fort and stone masonry dam. After A.K. Sharma's excavations in the early 1990s, it also came to be recognized as an important stone age site. The thousands of palaeolithic tools found here showed that this was both a huge habitation site as well as a factory site (i.e. a place where tools were made). We can note that traces of several palaeo-channels (ancient courses) of the Yamuna river have been identified nearby.

Important additions to the knowledge of Delhi's prehistory do not necessarily depend on large-scale excavations conducted by official agencies. A great deal can be achieved through a thorough surface investigation, even by a single individual. An example I would like to cite are the recent discoveries made by Mudit Trivedi, an MA student of Jawaharlal Nehru University (and I may proudly add, a former student of mine). Mudit's search for the prehistory of the JNU campus led to his discovery of several palaeoliths, microliths, and other interesting remains including a semicircular alignment of stones and petroglyphs. Clearly, the Delhi area is rich in prehistoric remains and the search for stone tools needs to be intensified. So look out for that hand-axe when you go for your morning walk on the ridge!

Let's go on to proto-historic remains. Most people know about the Harappan or Indus civilization (c. 2600–1900 BC). Archaeologists understand this culture as having an early, mature and late phase. The mature phase is when the cities and writing became established. The late Harappan phase is the post-urban phase, when cities and city life declined, roughly between 2000 BC and 1000 BC. Many late Harappan sites have been found in Haryana and western Uttar Pradesh. Late Harappan pottery has been identified at a few places in the Delhi area—Kharkhari Nahar (a village near Najafgarh in west Delhi) and Nachauli in Faridabad. Bhorgarh and Mandoli are two sites where late Harappan remains have been found in the course of archaeological excavations.

Bhorgarh is a village near Narela in north Delhi. Today the Yamuna is 10 km away but, in ancient times, the river flowed close by the site. A team of the Department of Archaeology of the Delhi Government led by B.S.R. Babu excavated the site between 1992 and 1994. The excavations revealed an occupation from the late Harappan phase to the medieval period. The late Harappan levels gave evidence of thick red pottery and graves.

Mandoli is a small village on the left bank of the Yamuna, near Nand Nagari in east Delhi. Excavations by the Department of Archaeology of the Delhi government in 1987-88 and 1988 89 at the site revealed occupation from the late Harappan phase to the fourth-fifth centuries AD. The late Harappan settlement here was fairly small. No structures survived, but there were remains of house floors made of rammed earth, marked by post-holes arranged in a circular or arc-fashion. Traces of a hearth (chullah) were found on one of the floors. The wheel-made pottery included jars with splayed out or beaded rims and vases with disc bases. A bead and a terracotta cake (the precise function of which is uncertain) were also found. The late Harappan settlement at Mandoli was washed away by floods.

Let's now move to the Purana Qila, the sixteenth century fort built by Humayun and Sher Shah. Those of you who have been here will have noticed that after buying your entry ticket at the ticket booth, you have to climb a slope to get to the gate. This is because the fort rests on a mound, which marks the site of an ancient settlement. Between 1954 and 1971, archaeologists conducted excavations here. As I mentioned earlier, there is unfortunately no full report of the discoveries, just snippets of information. The cultural sequence at the Purana Qila extended from about the fourth /third century BC to the Mughal period. The discovery of sherds of pottery known as Painted Grey Ware (PGW) on the surface suggests that the antiquity of the site may go back to c. 1000 BC.

According to popular belief, the legendary city of Indraprastha of Mahabharata fame was located at the Purana Qila. This link rests on local traditions, the earliest written account of which belongs to the medieval period. Abul Fazl's *Ain-i-Akbari* contains a synopsis of the Mahabharata events and tells us that Delhi was first called Indrapat. It also states that Humayun restored the citadel of Indrapat and named it Dinpanah. Till the end of the nineteenth century, a village called Indrapat was in fact located within the walls of the Purana Qila.

Excavations at other sites connected with the Mahabharata story such as Hastinapur, Panipat, Baghpat and Kurukshetra have also yielded Painted Grey Ware. All this neither proves nor disproves the historicity of the Mahabharata events. In fact, archaeology cannot give definite answers to the sorts of questions people often want answers to. What the archaeological evidence does show is that various sites connected with the Mahabharata story were inhabited from about 1000 BC onwards and that they shared a similar material culture.

Let's move on to the early historical period. During this

time, Delhi was located on a major artery of the great northern trade route known as the Uttarapatha. Remains associated with Northern Black Polished Ware (NBPW) pottery (seventh to second/first century BC) have been found at various places, including the Purana Qila. Some remains of the period c. 200 BC–200 AD have also been found at this site.

In 1996, a team of archaeologists of the Department of Archaeology of the Government of Delhi led by B.S.R. Babu conducted excavations at Jhatikara, about 12 km south of Najafgarh. The mound here was originally spread over some three acres, by now mostly destroyed and converted into fields. At the lower levels of the deposit, archaeologists found remains of mud brick structures that included a room with a hearth made of baked clay, a vase in a pit, a saddle quern (used for grinding food) and some miniature pots. The room seems to have been a kitchen belonging to the early centuries AD. A large number of potsherds, mostly wheel-made, were also unearthed at the site. The most common vessel was a bowl with a slightly incurved rim and heavy base. Fragments of vases of different sizes including ones with spouts, a basin with a sturdy rim and carinated handis were also found. Other discoveries included seven copper coins, two copper ear ornaments, one copper ring, a hoard of eighty-two terracotta beads, glass bangles, an animal figurine and several iron nails.

The more visible remains of the early historical period in Delhi are the Ashokan edicts: There are three sets of Ashokan edicts in Delhi today. Only one of them is in situ (i.e. in its original place). This is the Ashokan rock edict on Raja Dhir Singh Marg, near the ISKCON temple. It is known as the Bahapur or Srinivaspuri edict, though since it actually falls within East of Kailash, it should be known as the East of Kailash edict. The rock bears a version of Minor Rock Edict 1. Ashoka speaks in the first person. He tells us that he became a lay Buddhist two and a half years earlier, but confesses that initially he did not make much progress. He goes on to say that over a year ago, he had drawn closer to the Buddhist monastic order. He boasts that due to his efforts and exertions in promoting dhamma (piety), gods and men had come to mingle on earth. He describes dhamma as a goal that is not confined to the great and exalted but also open to humble folk, who can thereby attain heaven. The emperor exhorts the humble and the rich, as well as people living beyond the borders of his kingdom, to follow dhamma. The inscription ends with the king expressing his hope that the cause of dhamma would grow and endure forever.

Both the Ashokan pillars that stand today in Delhi were brought here by Firoz Shah Tughlaq in the fourteenth century. The Delhi–Topra pillar stands on top of a three-storeyed structure in Feroz Shah Kotla. Its smooth shaft has a number of inscriptions. Apart from seven edicts on dhamma inscribed during the reign of the Maurya emperor Ashoka, it has three twelfth century inscriptions of the Chauhan Rajput king Visaladeva alias Vigraharaja IV. There are also two sixteenth century inscriptions, one of which is in mixed Sanskrit and Persian and refers to Sultan Ibrahim, who may be identified with the sixteenth century Lodi king of that name. The Delhi–Meerut pillar stands opposite Bara Hindu Rao Hospital near the old Subzi Mandi. It has six Ashokan edicts on dhamma, below which are three short early fourteenth century Sanskrit inscriptions. Let's leave the Ashokan pillars at this point—we will return to them later.

The most impressive relic of the Gupta period (c. 300–600 AD) in the Delhi area is the iron pillar which today stands in the Jami Masjid in the Qutb complex in Mehrauli. The solid pillar, with its slightly tapering shaft, stands 7.16 m tall, and weighs about 6100 kg. It is surmounted by an inverted lotus emblem, over which there are three fluted discs (*amalakas*) supporting a square pedestal. This must have once been surmounted by a Vaishnava emblem, perhaps a *garuda*. The earliest inscription on the pillar evokes the memory of a great king in beautiful poetic Sanskrit. There is no date and no genealogy. Most historians consider it to be a *prashasti* (eulogy) of the fourth century Gupta king, Chandragupta II (375–413 AD), although Samudragupta is also a contender.

The inscription clearly suggests that the iron pillar was originally connected with a Vishnu temple.

Chemical analysis has shown that the pillar, the forging of which must have involved great metallurgical skill, is made of pure wrought iron with a very low sulphur and very high phosphorus content. The most special thing about this pillar is supposed to be the fact that it has remained comparatively rust-free even after so many centuries. I say comparatively because there *is* evidence of rusting on the areas where it has been exposed to prolonged contact with water—at the top and under the ground. Like the Ashokan pillars, the iron pillar has several short inscriptions. One of these refers to the Tomara Rajput king Anangapala establishing Delhi in the eleventh century.

We do not know for sure where the iron pillar originally stood. Most historians believe that it is not in situ. The inscription refers to a hill named Vishnupada; today there are no hills in the area. One suggestion is that Vishnupada was in the Himalayas, close to the source of the Beas river. Other suggestions are that the pillar was originally located at Udayagiri in central India or Gaya in Bihar. It is also possible that it was located somewhere else in the Mehrauli area itself. If it was moved here from somewhere else, who moved it? It may have been brought here by Anangapala Tomara. On the other hand, it has also been suggested that the pillar may have been installed in its present location by Sultan Iltutmish in the early thirteenth century, when the Qutb mosque was enlarged.

The Gupta iron pillar is connected with a colourful legend of how the city of Delhi got its name. One version of the story, recounted in the twelfth century *Prithviraja Raso*, speaks of a learned Brahman who told the Rajput king Bilan Deo or Anangapala Tomara that the pillar was immovable, that its base rested on the hood of Vasuki, the king of the serpents, and that the king's rule would last as long as the pillar stood firm. Anangapala was curious. He had the pillar dug out. The lower part was smeared with the blood of the serpent. The king realized his mistake and ordered that the pillar be put back into the ground. But no matter how hard his men tried, the pillar remained loose (*dhili*). And this, according to legend, is how the city of Dilli got its name!

Let's now go back to the Ashokan pillars, this time to track their adventures in medieval and modern times. As I mentioned earlier, both pillars were brought to Delhi in the fourteenth century, by Firoz Shah Tughlaq. Shams Siraj Afif writes in his *Tarikh-i-Firuz Shahi* that one was originally located in Tobra or Topra village (in modern Haryana) and the other near Meerut (in modern Uttar Pradesh). The Sultan chose the location of both pillars with care. He had the Topra pillar erected in the inner citadel of Firozabad near the banks of the Yamuna, while the Meerut pillar was installed in the royal hunting palace.

Afif describes how the Topra pillar—given the beautiful name of Minar-i-Zarin—was moved by a specially-constructed cart and then by boat from Topra to Delhi, and how it was installed on top of the three-storeyed structure at Firozabad. These details are supplemented by those in an anonymous Persian text of the same time called the *Sirat-i-Firuz Shahi*. Interestingly, a manuscript of the *Sirat* actually has illustrations showing the various stages of the operations. The texts hardly give any details of the moving of the Delhi–Meerut pillar. Was this because the pillar wasn't as impressive? Was it because it was installed in a less prominent and less prestigious location? Or was it because the procedure involved in moving and installing it was more or less the same as in the case of the Topra pillar and the medieval chroniclers did not consider it necessary to repeat the description?

The significance of the location of the Topra pillar in the Sultan's citadel, in direct line with its Jami Masjid, is abundantly clear. The location of the Delhi–Meerut pillar clearly had something to do with a nearby two-storeyed structure on the northern ridge, variously known as the Kushk-i-Shikar, Pirghaib, Jahanuma or the Observatory. Afif states that the pillar was set up in the Kushk-i-Shikar and that the same sorts of contrivances used to move and erect the Minar-i-Zarin also applied to the Meerut pillar. We are also told that the day the Meerut pillar was erected was celebrated with feasting and public rejoicings and glasses of sherbet did the rounds. The Ridge must have been heavily forested then. Having taken the trouble to bring the pillar to his Hunting Palace, would the Sultan not have wanted to display it appropriately by elevating it, so that it could be seen and admired from afar? We really don't know whether the pillar was embedded on an elevated ground (the Kushk does stand on the highest point of this part of the Ridge), or on the Kushk-i-Shikar, or perhaps even on some other structure nearby. I wish I could prove that the pillar was once located on *top* of the Pirghaib structure. The problem is that we don't know exactly what the original structure looked like and whether it could have taken the weight of the pillar. We can only speculate.

The Delhi–Meerut pillar was clearly part of a complex of structures built on this part of the northern Ridge during the time of Firoz Shah Tughlaq. About fifty yards to the south west of the Pirghaib are the remains of a huge baoli made of rubble masonry, with traces of rooms around it, ascribed to the reign of this king. The baoli must have provided water to the Kushk. It has also been suggested that the origins of the Chauburja not far away also go back to the time of Firoz Shah, although the present form of the structure shows late Mughal features.

The sites chosen for the installation of the Ashokan pillars clearly indicate that they had an important symbolic significance for Firoz Shah. The fact that they were considered marvels is clear from the following extract from the *Sirat-i-Firuz Shahi*, translated from the Persian by Mohammad Hamid Kuraishi:

> This pillar, high as heaven, is made of a single block of stone and tapers upward, being broad at the base and narrow at the top.

> Seen from a hundred *farsang* (anywhere between 2½-8 miles) it looks like a hillock of gold, as the Sun when it spreads its rays in the morning.
> No bird—neither eagle, nor crane—can fly as high as its top; and arrows, whether khadang (made of poplar) or khatai (arrows from khata), cannot reach its middle.
> If thunder were to rage about the top of this pillar, no one could hear the sound owing to the great distance (between the top of the pillar and the ground).
> O God! How did they lift this heavy mountain (i.e. the pillar)? and in what did they fix it (so firmly) that it does not move from its place?
> How did they carry it to the top of the building which almost touches the heavens and place it there (in its upright position)?
> How could they paint it all over with gold, (so beautifully) that it appears to the people like the golden morning! . . .
>
> . . . And truly as the removal of the stone monolith and its erection in front of the mosque by the order of the King is a wonderful achievement, the methods employed in its removal and erection are being recorded in this book, in order that the description may be useful for those who wish to know the details thereof . . .

It is possible that the pillar was originally thought to have had a religious significance. This is suggested by the *Sirat*, which refers to it having been connected with a temple. Furthermore, the text very emphatically emphasizes that Sultan Firoz Shah was to be given full credit for the operations, from beginning to end. It says that the king urged the engineers and all the wise men of the time to come up with a plan, but they couldn't.

The Ashokan pillars must have caught Firoz Shah's attention due to the technical skill involved in making them, their beauty, majesty, perhaps also their mystery. The older inscriptions on their shafts could not be read at the time, but the later ones could. This is clear from the fact that the *Sirat* mentions that one of the inscriptions belonged to the reign of the Chauhan king Visaladeva. In an unknowing, uncanny way, a medieval king had connected himself with one of the most celebrated kings of ancient India!

The modern history of the Delhi–Meerut pillar is even more turbulent than its medieval history. Alexander Cunningham writes that in the 1860s, the pillar lay in five pieces near Hindu Rao's house on the top of a hill on the Delhi ridge. The site of this house is now marked by Bara Hindu Rao Hospital; some of the old parts of the building can still be identified. The pillar is said to have been broken into pieces due to the accidental explosion of a magazine of gun-powder in the early eighteenth century, during the reign of the Mughal king Farukhsiyar. Its pieces were presented by Hindu Rao to the museum of the Asiatic Society of Bengal. One part, inscribed with Ashoka's edicts, was sawn off by the executive engineer of Delhi and despatched to Calcutta. In 1866, it was returned to Delhi and the pieces joined together.

The Kushk-i-Shikar is today associated with a *pir* (Sufi master). When I visited it in early 2006, the northern room on the first floor, which has a cenotaph, had a prominently placed metal stand with agarbattis (incense sticks). Next to this was an empty glass bottle, diyas and genda flowers. The cenotaph was covered by a green chadar with gold zari. Next to this was a small red-and-gold cloth, on it a small murti of Lakshmi. The first floor landing was being used for more utilitarian purposes—such as drying red chillies and providing birds of thc arca with watcr. The cenotaph covered with the chadar had recently placed offerings of incense sticks and flowers. Further, a Baba comes here every Thursday and offers advice to a regular, faithful following.

Interesting things are also going on at the structure which supports the Ashokan pillar in Firoz Shah Kotla. When I visited it in early 2006, incense sticks marked the blackened walls of its many niches, in which were stuck numerous petitions related to a host of personal problems addressed to Kotwali

Baba or Dada Miyan. Believers consider the three-storey stone structure at Firoz Shah Kotla to be inhabited by many *jinns*, the most important of whom is known as 'Lat-wale-Baba' (the Baba of the pillar).

The fascinating life histories of the Ashokan pillars and the Gupta period iron pillar show us how some historical remains take on new roles and meanings in later times. Another example of this phenomenon can be seen in many old villages in the Delhi area, where fragments of old sculptures can be seen assembled under trees in village shrines dedicated to *grama-devatas* or *khera-devatas*. Reconstructing such long-term histories allows us to make fascinating journeys across time. It shows us how the ancient past gets entwined with the medieval and the modern, often in unexpected, surprising ways.

William Dalrymple

Religious Rhetoric in the Delhi Uprising of 1857

The uprising of 1857 produced one or two impeccably secular declarations. The much-quoted Azimgarh proclamation, for example, an Avadhi production of late August 1857 and issued by the young prince Feroz Shah, is the nearest thing produced during the Uprising to a manifesto of national independence. Its opening sentence sets the tone, a cry to arms noting that 'both Hindoos and Mohammedans are being ruined under the tyranny and oppression of the infidel and treacherous English'. While noting that 'at present a war is ranging with the English on account of religion', and calling on 'pundits and fakirs' to join with Mughal armies, most of its space is given over to complaints that the English have overtaxed the landowners, monopolized 'all the posts of dignity and emolument' in the civil and armed services and put Indian artisans out of business by flooding the market with cheap British imports.

Yet what is striking about so many of the public proclamations coming out of the uprising's storm centre of Delhi during 1857 was the emphatically religious articulation that the documents take on all sides of the conflict. In Delhi there is little talk about textile imports or land tenure or taxation, at least in the surviving public proclamations of the rebels. Instead the overwhelming theme of the rhetoric of the

Delhi uprising centred around the threat that the Company posed to religion. This is not to say that there were not many deeply felt, very concrete and thoroughly secular grievances. Yet the public declarations concerned only one thing: as the sepoys told Zafar on 11 May 1857, 'We have joined hands to protect our religion and our faith'.[1] Later they stood in Chandni Chowk, the main street of Delhi, and asked people: 'Brothers: are you with those of the faith?'[2] British men and women who had converted to Islam—and there were a surprising number of those in Delhi—were not hurt; but Indians who had converted to Christianity were cut down immediately.

Even if one accepts that the word 'religion' (for Muslims' din) is often being used in the very general and non-sectarian sense of dharma (or duty, righteousness)—so that when the sepoys saying they are rising to defend their dharma, they mean as much their way of life as their sectarian religious identity—it is still highly significant that the Urdu sources from Delhi repeatedly refer to the British not as angrez (the English) or as goras (whites) or even firangis (foreigners, Franks), but instead almost always as kafirs (infidels) and nasrani (Christians).

The Court

In particular the tone of the letters and petitions and proclamations issued from the Mughal court in 1857 is overwhelmingly religious in subject matter: over and over again we are told '*Yeh laray mazhab ke liye shuru huee*' or, at other times '*Yeh laray din ke liye shuru huee*'. Yet the religious language is expressed in such a way that is clearly and explicitly inclusive of both Hindus and Muslims, as one would expect from the court at this period.

Zafar's eldest surviving legitimate son Mirza Mughal was almost certainly behind a circular letter sent out in Zafar's name to all the princes and rajahs of India, asking them to join the uprising and appealing for their loyalty on the grounds that all faiths were under attack by the British. The letter refers specifically to the laws banning sati and allowing converts to inherit, and the Company's facilitation of missionary activity and the alleged conversion of prisoners locked in British jails: 'The English are people who overthrow all religions,' it states. 'You should understand well their object of destroying the religions of Hindustan . . . It is now my firm conviction that if the English continue in Hindustan they will . . . utterly overthrow our religions. As the English are the common enemy of both [Hindus and Muslims, we] should unite in considering their slaughter . . . for by this alone will the lives and faiths of both be saved.'[3]

Maulvi Muhammed Baqir, the outspoken editor of the *Dihli Urdu Akbhar* and father of the Urdu poet and critic Muhammad Husain Azad, echoed this vision in slightly different and more explicitly Islamic language. At the outbreak of the Rising, in May 1857 he wrote in his columns how the rebellion had been sent by God to punish the kafirs for their arrogant plan to wipe out the religions of India. For him the speed and thoroughness of the reverse suffered by the British was proof of miraculous divine intervention, and it was no surprise therefore that such an event should be accompanied by dreams and visions:

> One venerable man had a dream that our Prophet Mohammed, Praise Be Upon Him, said to Jesus that your followers have become an enemy of my name and wish to efface my religion. To this Lord Jesus replied that the British are not my followers, they do not follow my path, they have joined ranks with Satan's followers . . . Some people even swear that the day the troopers came here, there were camels ahead of them on which rode green-robed riders . . . These green riders instantly vanished from sight and only the troopers remained, killing whichever Englishman they found, cutting them up as if they were carrots or radishes . . . Truly the English have been afflicted with divine wrath by the

true avenger. Their arrogance has brought them divine retribution for, as the Holy Koran says, "God does not love the arrogant ones".[4]

No less excited by the new turn of events was Baqar's twenty-seven-year-old son, Muhammad Husain, later to become famous as the poet Azad. The second edition of the paper to be published after the arrival of the sepoys in Delhi, that of 24 May, contained Azad's first published poem, entitled *A History of Instructive Reversals*. The ghazals began with a series of rhetorical questions: Where now was the empire of Alexander? Where the realm of Solomon? before moving on to the fate of the Christian empire in India:

Yesterday the Christians were in the ascendant,
World-seizing, world-bestowing,
The possessors of skill and wisdom,
The possessors of splendour and glory
The possessors of a mighty army.
But what use was that,
Against the sword of the Lord of Fury?
All their wisdom could not save them,
Their schemes became useless,
Their knowledge and science availed them nothing
The Telingas of the East have killed them all.
O Azad, learn this lesson:
For all their wisdom and vision,
The Christian rulers have been erased,
Without leaving a trace in this world.[5]

Even Zafar articulated the Uprising as a religious war:

As late as 6 September, at the very end of the siege when calling the people of Delhi to rally against the coming assault by the British, a proclamation issued in the name of Zafar spelled out very plainly 'that this is a religious war, and is being prosecuted on account of the faith, and it behoves all Hindus and Musalman residents of the imperial city, or of the villages in the country . . . to continue true to their faith and creeds.'[6]

The Mujahedin

A quite different tone emerges from the rhetoric of the groups of Muslim fighters who identified themselves in their petitions as mujahedin or ghazis.

It needs of course to be stated that the concept of jihad is a richly ambiguous one, that it varies according to context, and that the struggle referred to can take many forms. It is also true that the term mujahedin can refer to a variety of different kinds of volunteer. Moreover, we find on occasion the term jihad being used at this period by and about Hindus, so in Delhi in the Mutiny Papers we find two of the Hindu sepoy generals, Generals Sudhari and Hira Singh using the term to describe their fight against the British.

Nevertheless, when the Delhi sources of 1857 refer to the mujahedin and the Ghazis they are referring quite explicitly to the armed Muslim groups that arrived at Delhi—made up of a ragtag assortment of 'Wahhabi' maulvis, militant Naqshandis and, most numerous of all, pious Muslim civilians—especially 'weavers, artisans and other wage earners'—who believed it was their duty to free what they regarded as the *Dar ul-Islam* from the rule of the kafirs [infidels], and some of whom are explicit in their wish to seek martyrdom.[7]

Some mujahedin were already in Delhi before the outbreak. By the end of the third day of the Uprising, so many of the richest havelis had been broken into and looted, usually with the excuse that the inhabitants were sheltering Christians, that Mufti Sadruddin Azurda helped form a private police force to protect himself and his circle. The men he turned to were the only Delhiwallahs with sufficient arms and military training to take on the sepoys. These were the fighters of the underground mujahedin network that seems to have survived on the trading route linking Peshawar, Tonk, Delhi and Patna since the time of Sayyid Ahmed Barelvi, a brotherhood, bound to fight the jihad by oaths of allegiance (or *bayat)* to a leader (or *amir*). These now cast off their veil of secrecy and began to mass in Delhi, ready for the holy war they had so long prepared for.

According to Jawan Lal's diary, the mujahedin force was operational by 15 May. During the trial of Azurda at the end of the Uprising, the three commanders of his jihadi guard were named—'Abd ur-Rahman Ludhianawi, his son Sayf ur-Rahman and Muhammad Munir—and the reasons for their employment were discussed in court. Later in the uprising these jihadis did succeed in fending off an attack on Azurda's house, according to Jawan Lal: 'The house of Moulvie Sadar-ud-din Khan was attacked today by fifty soldiers; but, seeing that there were seventy jihadis ready to oppose them, they retreated, but carried off two colts from the house of Ahsanullah Khan.' Even more unequivocal is the report of Azurda's refusing a demand for money, saying that the ghazis he had employed would be used for his defence.

Four hundred men identified in the Delhi sources as mujahedin and ghazis marched in during the first week of the siege from nearby Gurgaon, Hansi and Hissar, but much the largest contingent—well over 4,000 strong—came from the small Muslim principality of Tonk in Rajasthan, which had a history of welcoming Wahhabi preachers, and which had been regarded by British intelligence officers as the centre of an underground centre of the mujahedin movement since the time of Sayyid Ahmed Barelvi.

On arrival the mujahedin set up camp both in the courtyard of the Jama Masjid, and that of the riverside Zinat ul-Masajid, the most beautiful of all the Delhi mosques. It is a measure of the distrust and tension between the sepoys and mujahedin that although they often fought side by side, the sepoys seem nonetheless to have regularly searched individuals going in and out of both mosques, and detained several people whom they regarded as suspicious.[8]

In contrast to the notably inclusive language of the court, mujahedin documents are sometimes nakedly communal. On 19 May, one of the more orthodox imams of Delhi, Maulvi Muhammad Sayyid, set up a standard of jihad in the Jama Masjid, in an apparent effort to turn the uprising into an exclusively Muslim Holy War. Zafar immediately ordered it to be taken down 'because such a display of fanaticism would only tend to exasperate the Hindus.'

The next day, just as news came that the Delhi Field Force was collecting in Ambala, the maulvi turned up at the palace to remonstrate with Zafar, claiming that the Hindus were all supporters of the English, and that a jihad against them was therefore perfectly legitimate. At the same time a delegation of Delhi Hindus also turned up at the fort, angrily denying the maulvi's charge. Zafar declared that in his eyes Hindus and Muslims were equal and that 'such a jihad is quite impossible, and such an idea an act of extreme folly, for the majority of the Purbeah soldiers were Hindus. Such an act would create internecine war and the results would be deplorable. The Holy War is against the English,' said Zafar emphatically. 'I have forbidden it against the Hindus.'[9]

The mujahedin and their firebrand maulvis calling for jihad in the city's mosques did however appeal to a few of Delhi's Muslims; the people of Delhi, however, remained dubious about the pleasure of hosting several thousand holy warriors. This was especially so given the far from friendly attitude of the mujahedin towards Delhi's Hindus—half the city's population—and the importance the Delhi elite placed on not upsetting the delicate equilibrium between Hindus and Muslims in the city: 'Their stated object was a crusade against the infidel,' wrote Sa'id Mubarak Shah, 'their real one was plunder. In this manner, fully five thousand men from various quarters poured into Delhi as ghazees, the majority armed with *gundasahs* [battle axes] and dressed in blue tunics and green turbans.'[10]

Such was the coolness of the reception given to the

mujahedin that it was not long before one of their maulvis came before Zafar to complain that they were being unjustly neglected: 'We Mujahedin have displayed great valour and dedication but until now we have received no appreciation for it, nor has there even been any enquiries as to how we have fared . . . We only hope that our services will be recognised and rewarded, so we will be able to continue to participate in the battle.'[11]

A similar petition came a fortnight later, from a man who described himself as the Principal Risaldar of the Tonk mujahedin. In his case the complaint was more serious: his jihadis had been deserted by the sepoys during an assault and left to take on the kafir infidels all by themselves:

> We joined in the attack yesterday, and 18 infidels were despatched to Hell by your slave's own hands, and five of his followers were killed and five wounded. Your Majesty, the rest of the army gave us no help whilst we were engaged in combat with the infidels. Had they even made a show of support, as was to have been expected, with the help of Providence a complete victory yesterday would have been achieved . . . I trust that now some arms, together with some trifling funds, may be bestowed on my followers, so that they might have the strength to fight and slay the infidels, and so realize their desires.

Considering this, it is hardly surprising that there is evidence of tension, not only between the mujahedin and the people of Delhi, but also between the sepoys and the mujahedin. Occasionally the tension between the overwhelmingly Hindu sepoys and the militantly Muslim mujahedin erupted into full-scale street fights.[12]

Towards the end of July the jihadis made the most serious breach in the common front that had been so successfully maintained by both Hindus and Muslims. The feast of Bakr

'Id was approaching; to the horror of the court, who had always made huge efforts never to allow the city to be divided on communal grounds, the jihadis went out of their way deliberately to offend Hindu feelings. As Mohammad Baqar wrote:

> The Ghazees who have come from Tonk have determined to kill a cow on the open space in front of the Jama Masjid on the day of 'Id, some three days hence. They say that if the Hindus offer any opposition to this, they will kill them, and after settling accounts with the Hindus they will then attack and destroy the firangis, 'For,' say they, 'we are to be martyrs for the faith and the honours of martyrdom are to be obtained just as well by killing a Hindu as by killing a firangi.'[13]

Shortly afterwards, on 19 July, some Hindu sepoys cut the throats of five Muslim butchers they accused of cow killing. A full-scale crisis, dividing the city down its central religious axis, looked imminent. This was something Zafar had always dreaded. Since Delhi was almost exactly half Hindu, he had always clearly understood that it would be impossible to rule without the consent and blessing of half his subjects; moreover he had a Hindu mother, and had always followed enough Hindu customs to profoundly alarm the more orthodox ulama.

Now he rose to the occasion with an unusually decisive response. The same day as the butchers were killed, Zafar banned the butchery of cows, forbade the eating of beef, and authorised for anyone found killing a cow the terrible punishment of being blown from a cannon. The police reacted immediately, even going so far as to arrest any kebab wallah who was found grilling beef kebabs. One of these, Hafiz Abdurrahman, wrote to the court swearing that he was not a butcher and could not be held responsible for cow slaughter; moreover he had only taken up his current profession of kebab grilling after his usual business had been ruined by the rioting of the sepoys. He was not, however, released.[14]

Next, Zafar issued an order that all the town's cows should be registered, with chaukidars and sweepers of the different muhallas instructed to report to the local police station all 'cow-owning Muslim households', and for each police thana then to make out a list 'of all the cows being bred by the followers of Islam' and to send it to the palace. The thanadars were instructed to carry out this order within six hours.[15] On 30 May, the Kotwal, Sa'id Mubarak Shah, was instructed to proclaim loudly throughout the town that cow killing was absolutely forbidden since it would cause 'unnecessary strife which will only strengthen the enemy'; anyone 'who even harbours the thought or acts in defiance of the government order will receive severe punishment.'[16]

Further orders followed, including one oddly surreal directive commanding that all the registered cows should now be given shelter in the central city's police station, the Kotwali. Zafar may have been unwilling or unable to lock up the jihadis, but he could lock up the cows.

Throughout all this, there is evidence that the Delhi elite were seriously worried by the possibility of a split developing between the Delhi Hindus and Muslims. Things came to such a pass that Maulvi Muhammad Baqar included in his columns of the *Delhi Urdu Akhbar* a call for the Hindus of the city not to lose heart—which of course implied that they were beginning to do just that. A remarkable letter aimed at his Hindu readers was included in Baqar's issue of 14 June. In it, he called for all Delhi's citizens to pull together against the common British enemy, whom he compared to Ravana, the demon king.

'O my countrymen,' he wrote,

> Looking at the strategy and devious cleverness of the English, their ability to make arrangements and to order the world in the way they wish, the wide expanses of

their dominions and their overflowing treasuries and revenues, you may feel disheartened that such a people could ever be overcome. But my Hindu brothers, if you look in your Holy books you will see how many magnificent dynasties have come into being in the land of Hindustan, and how they all met their end. Even Ravana and his army of demons were beaten by Raja Ramchandra [the Hindu God King Ram] . . . Except the Adipurush, the primaeval Deity, nothing is permanent . . .

If God brings all these magnificent kingdoms to an end after a short period, why do you not comprehend that God has sent his hidden help [to defeat] this hundred year old kingdom [of the British] so that this community [the Christians] who regarded the children of God with contempt, and addressed your brothers and sisters as 'black men,' have now been insulted and humiliated? Realise this, and you will lose your fear and apprehension. To run away and turn your back now would be akin to denying divine help and favour . . . [17]

The Hindus

Hindus too, though more elusive in the Delhi documents, had their leaders who turned to the scriptures to encourage their people to fight. One Brahmin in particular, Pandit Harichandra seems to have been particularly prominent and appears in several British intelligence reports: 'He tells the officers,' reported one spy:

that by virtue of his astrological and esoteric arts he has learned that the divine forces will support the army. He has named an auspicious day when he says there will be a terrifying fight, a new Kurukshetra [the battle at the climax of the Mahabharata] like the one between the Kauravas and the Pandavas of yore. He tells the sepoys that their horses' feet will be drenched in British blood and then the victory will be theirs. All the people in the army have great faith in him, so much so that the time and the place designated by the Pandit are chosen for the fighting.[18]

The Christians

But it was the religious rhetoric of the Christians which was arguably the most extreme of all.

India in the 1840s and 1850s was slowly filling with pious British Evangelicals who wanted not just to rule and administer India, but also to redeem and improve it. In Calcutta, Jennings' colleague Mr Edmunds was vocal in making known his belief that the Company should use its position more forcibly to bring about the conversion of India. 'The time appears to have come,' he wrote in a widely-read circular letter, 'when earnest consideration should be given to the subject, whether or not all men should embrace the same system of religion. Railways, steam vessels and the electric telegraph are rapidly uniting all the nations of the earth . . . The land is being leavened and Hinduism is being everywhere undermined. Great will some day, in God's appointed time, be the fall of it.'[19]

Nor was it any longer just the missionaries who dreamt of converting India. To the north-west of Delhi, the Commissioner of Peshawar, Herbert Edwards, firmly believed an empire had been given to Britain because of the virtues of English Protestantism: 'The Giver of Empires is indeed God,' he wrote, and He gave the Empire to Britain because 'England had made the greatest effort to preserve the Christian religion in its purest apostolic form.'[22]

Worst of all was Rev. John Midgely Jennings, the British chaplain who installed himself in chambers inside the Lahore Gate of the Red Fort from which he poured forth a stream of explicitly anti-Hindu and Islamophobic pamphlets. The city of the Mughals, Jennings had concluded, was nothing less than a last earthly bastion of the Prince of Darkness himself: 'Within its walls,' he wrote,

> the pride of life, the lust of the eye and all the lusts of the flesh have reigned and revelled to the full, and all the glories of the Kingdoms of this portion of the earth have passed from one wicked possessor to another. It is as though it were permitted the Evil One there at least to verify his boast that he giveth it to whom he will; but of truth, of meekness and of righteousness the power has not been seen . . .[21]

Jennings' plan was to rip up what he regarded as the false faiths of India, by force if necessary: 'The roots of ancient religions have here, as in all old places, struck deep and men must be able to fathom deep in order to uproot them.'[22] His method was simple: to harness the power of the rising British Empire—clearly the instrument 'of the mysterious sway of God's Providence'—towards converting the heathen.

The British Crown, argued Jennings in his prospectus for his proposed Delhi Mission, was now the proud possessor of the Koh-i-Noor diamond, once the property of the Mughals, India's greatest dynasty. In gratitude, the British should now endeavour in earnest to bring about the conversion of India and so 'give in return that "pearl of great price" [the Christian faith] . . . As the course of our Empire is so marvellously taking its course from the East of India towards its West,' so should the British be preparing to conquer the subcontinent for Anglicanism and the one true God.[23] There should, he believed, be no compromise with false religions.

In the course of the Uprising, and particularly after the slaughter of the British women and children both in Delhi and at Kanpur, this language grew more violent. George Wagentrieber was the editor of the *Delhi Gazette*, who escaped Delhi on 11 May and now invoked the Christian God in his editorials as he called for a bloody revenge: referring to the rebels as 'hell hounds', Wagentrieber says that they have 'executed thus far their diabolical scheme of raising once again the standard of the lascivious Prophet, in opposition to the new dispensation offered to mankind, in the man Christ Jesus, the son of God . . .'

> Hindoo and Moslem have proclaimed their caste and their religion to the world in a mass of fiendish cruelty that stands as unparalleled in the world's history. The punishment about to be inflicted will likewise be equivalent: Justice is Mercy— 'blood for blood' will be the watchword throughout the storm pending over the doomed city; the British soldier must hurry: the Avenging Angel uses you in the massacre that awaits your advance on Delhi.

As far as many of the British troops were concerned, their fury and thirst for revenge was not so much a desire as a right enshrined in the Bible. One British soldier, 'Quaker' Wallace, was in the habit of bayoneting his sepoy adversaries while chanting the 116th Psalm. As General Neill put it, 'The Word of God gives no authority to the modern tenderness for human life.'[24]

This was echoed by Padre Rotton, the chaplain of the Delhi Field Force. The rebels did not realise, he wrote, that the uprising was in fact

> 'a battle of principles, a conflict between truth and error; and that because they had elected in favour of darkness, and eschewed the light, therefore they could not possibly succeed. Moreover, they had imbrued their hands in the innocent blood of helpless women and children, and that very blood was [now] appealing to heaven for vengeance. The appeal was unquestionably heard. The Lord could not otherwise than be avenged on such a nation as this.'[25]

Conclusion

For all that the Uprising in Delhi was expressed in religious rhetoric, and for all that it continued to be represented as such by the participants as the siege of Delhi continued, reality and rhetoric came increasingly to diverge as the siege neared its end.

It was not religious principles but the lack of a generally agreed leadership that led to the failure of the defence of Delhi. None of the sepoys would take orders from the subedar of any other regiment, so they fought in a disconnected and uncoordinated fashion. On top of this there was a failure to gather intelligence, to coordinate effectively with other rebel centres such as Kanpur and Lucknow, or to persuade most of the independent rajahs of Central India and Rajputana to come off the fence and join with the cause.

But the rebellion was defeated as much because of the shortcomings of the rebels' administrative and financial organisation, as much as their military and strategic failures. They had created turbulence and chaos, but could not restore order. This was particularly fatal for them in the countryside around Delhi. Their failure to establish a well-governed 'liberated area' or Mughal realm from which they could draw tax revenue, manpower and most of all food supplies, ultimately proved the Delhi rebels' single most disastrous failure. No food was coming in, so prices rose dramatically, and starvation soon set in. By the time the British finally assaulted the city on 14 September, the number of sepoy defenders had sunk from a peak of 100,000 down to 25,000. Most left because of hunger: the rebel administration had failed to provide either food or pay or munitions.

As early as 7 June, even the employees of the Royal Household were complaining that they had received no rations for a month.[26] On 12 June, the deputy kotwal wrote to his assistants begging them to find some food for the new battalions from Haryana who had just marched into Delhi. At the bottom is the reply: 'It is submitted that there is nothing left in the shops, no flour, no pulses, nothing. What should we do?'[27] By 15 June, the officers of the different regiments were coming to the Fort and complaining that their troops could not attack the British on empty stomachs, and that their sepoys had begun returning, 'driven back by hunger before the battle is over.'[28]

Six weeks later, on 28 July, Kishan Dayal and Qadir Bahksh, Subahdars of the Meerut sepoys, came to court to say their men were now starving. They had left behind in Meerut all their possessions when they mutinied, 'so are now very hard pressed. Some eight-ten days have passed and we have not even received a single chick-pea. My men are dismayed at the expense of everything, and there are no money-lenders who will give them loans.'[29]

In contrast the British achieved victory for the same unromantic and unheroic reason they achieved victory almost everywhere else in India: they were famous for paying their troops as regularly as they promised. It was this that allowed them to recruit a brand new mercenary army from the Punjab and send it to the Delhi Ridge—a mercenary army that was for all the religious and jihadi rhetoric coming out of the besieged city—at least half Pathan and Punjabi Muslim.

At the beginning of the siege of Delhi, an all white Christian army faced a largely upper caste Hindu army of their former sepoys. By the end, the British had managed to recruit a new and religiously mixed army that defied the religious rhetoric on both sides: four-fifths of the so-called British army was Sikh, or Punjabi Muslim or Pathan; and facing them was the remnants of the sepoy army which had gathered in Delhi—perhaps as few as 25,000 of the original 100,000 sepoys along with what the British intelligence officers estimated as 25,000 of the mujahedin.

Every generation writes history that reflects the times in which they live. Marxist and nationalist historians, many of them proud atheists, writing after the freedom struggle emphasized the secular, social and economic nature of the grievances Indians had against the British, at least partly in reaction to the emphasis given by the Victorians to religious matters, and the tendency of the British to blame the entire Uprising on an entirely mythical 'international Muslim conspiracy' with links to Mecca and Tehran. But in our own time, after Ayodhya and 9/11, it is not difficult to feel that earlier generations have perhaps a little underplayed the power of faith and religion as a motivator and mover of men in 1857. Religion is not the only force at work, nor perhaps the primary one; but to ignore its power and importance, at least in the rhetoric used to justify the uprising, seems to go against the huge weight of emphasis on this factor given in the rebels' own documents.

Notes

1 Mutiny Papers, Collection 60, No. 830, National Archives of India (NAI hereafter).

2 The City of Delhi during 1857 (translation of the account of Said Mobarak Shah), Eur Mss B 138, Oriental and India Office Collections (British Libraries), (OIOC hereafter).

3 The letter was first printed in English in N.A. Chick, *Annals of the Indian Rebellion 1857–58* (Calcutta, 1859; reprinted London 1972), pp. 101–03. It has recently been reprinted in Salim al-Din Quraishi, *Cry for Freedom: Proclamations of Muslim Revolutionaries of 1857* (Lahore, 1997).

4 *Dihli Urdu Akbhar*, 17 May 1857.

5 This translation is my own colloquial reworking of the more literal translation given by Fran Pritchett in *Nets*, p. 24.

6 Quoted by the prosecution in the concluding speech at the trial of Zafar, *Proceedings on the Trial of Muhammad Bahadur Shah, Titular King of Delhi, before a Military Commission, upon a Charge of Rebellion, Treason and Murder, Held at Delhi, on the 27th Day of January 1858, and Following Days* (London, 1859), p. 142.

7 Irfan Habib, 'The Coming of 1857', *Social Scientist*, Vol. 26, No. 1, Jan–April 1998, p. 12.

8 See for example Mutiny Papers, Collection 67, No. 77, 27 July 1857, NAI, for Zinat ul-Masajid; and Collection 15, No. 1 for Jama Masjid.

9 *Two Native Narratives*: *Narrative of Munshi Jawan*, p. 98. There is another account of the same incident in *Trial of Bahadur Shah Zafar*, 'Narrative of Chuni Lal, Newswriter', p. 108.

10 'Account of Said Mobarak Shah', Eur Mss, B 138, OIOC.

11 Petition of Maulvi Sarfaraz Ali, 10 Sept 1857, Mutiny Papers, Collection 65, No. 36, NAI.

12 See, for example, Mutiny Papers, Collection 73, No. 171, NAI.

13 Mutiny Papers. File No. 5028, July 1857, DCO archive, New Delhi. Translation of a letter from Munshee Mahomed Bakar, Editor of the *Delhi Oordoo Akhbar*, 28 July.

14 Mutiny Papers, Collection 103, No. 132, 14 July 1857, NAI.

15 Mutiny Papers, Collection 45, 26 July 1857, NAI.

16 Mutiny Papers, Collection 111c, No.64, 30 July 1857, NAI.

17 *Dihli Urdu Akbhar,* 14 June 1857.

18 Mutiny Papers, Collection 15, No. 19, undated, NAI.

19 Derrick Hughes, *The Mutiny Chaplains* (Salisbury, 1991), p. 20.

20 Quoted by Charles Allen, *Soldier Sahibs: The Men Who Made the North-West Frontier* (London, 2000) p. 340.

21 'Proposed Mission at Delhi', Jennings Papers, Oxford, Bodleian Library of Commonwealth and African Studies at Rhodes House Missionary Collections (OBLCAS hereafter).

22 JMJ to Hawkins, 4 May 1852, Copies of Letters by the Revd Midgeley Jennings, Chaplain of Delhi 1851–57, Jennings Papers, OBLCAS.

23 'Proposed Mission at Delhi', Jennings Papers, OBLCAS.

24 Cited by Christopher Hibbert, *The Great Mutiny: India 1857*, pp. 201, 340

25 John Edward Rotton, *The Chaplain's Narrative of the Siege of Delhi* (London, 1858), p. 123

26 Abdul Latif, entry for 7 June, *1857 Ka Tarikhi Roznamacha*, ed. K.A. Nizami in *Naqwatul Musannifin* (Delhi, 1958).

27 Mutiny Papers, Collection 128, No. 39, 12 June 1857, NAI.

28 *Memoirs of Hakim Ahanullah Khan*, ed. by S. Moinul Haq (Karachi, 1958), p. 16.

29 Mutiny Papers, Collection 57, Nos. 185,186, 28 July 1857, NAI.

Sunil Kumar

The Pir's *Barakat* and the Servitor's Ardour: The Contrasting History of Two Sufi Shrines in Delhi

Delhi's landscape is dotted with the ruins of forts, mosques, tombs and minarets of all sizes constructed at different times by the Sultans of Delhi (1192–1526) or, somewhat later, by the Mughal Emperors and their courtiers (1526–1857). They provide the city with a sense of grandeur, dignity and history—the country's Independence Day celebrations are heralded from the ramparts of one such medieval monument. It is curious then, that the epithet for the city most frequently encountered in medieval sources—Hazrat-i Dehli or the auspicious, sacred city—is derived not so much by the derring-dos of this bunch of heroes but by another body of elites: mystics, theologians, litterateurs and jurists who made this city their place of residence. The epithet, Hazrat-i Dehli, was first used by the jurist and chronicler Minhaj-i Siraj Juzjani to describe the marvellous qualities of the city which, in the 1220s and 1230s, provided sanctuary to the literati and the pious from Transoxiana, Iran and Afghanistan, fleeing from the Mongol invasions of Chinggis Khan.

Their significance in the unfolding history of the city notwithstanding, few histories of Delhi concern themselves about these people. This might be because the architectural remnants of their presence are not nearly as grandiose as those of the temporal monarchs of the age. Their tombs, grave shrines, sometimes small mausoleums occupy spaces in the interstices of the sepulchres of the mighty lords of the time and the towering fortifications of their capitals. Many of these sites are unmarked and, in their anonymity, completely lost to history. Many others are in disrepair, with their Persian and Arabic inscriptions unreadable, some currently in use as toilets by the burgeoning street population of the capital. But there are others that take your breath away, not by their Taj Mahal-like grandeur, but by the intensity of spiritual emotion, the bustle of life, the colour, sound and noise that soaks their precincts. The nuclei of all these arenas are old graves but to the pilgrims who arrive to pay obeisance at their side, these are holy sites—the final resting places of their spiritual masters (*pir*) who provide them with guidance and succour in their difficult passages through life. His grace (*barakat*) imbues the premise, turning his grave into a *mazar,* a centre of pilgrimage. These are friends of God (*auliya*) and although physically absent, their spirit is manifest to their followers which is why they refer to him as *zinda pir*, the living master.

The contrast between the grave sites of Sultans, Padshahs and zinda pirs cannot be starker. In the former, the attention of the visitor is riveted by the adorned grave or the architectural beauty of the mausoleums. By contrast, at a mazar it is rarely the architecture that draws our attention; instead it is the simple *chadar* covered grave and the rituals of the servitor of the shrine (*sajjada nishin*), the servants (*khadims*) and the devotion of the pilgrims that overwhelm us. Neither the crowd nor the smells are terribly romantic or appealing by themselves. But they are an entrancing, embracing mixture when taken together with the mood of general expectancy and excitement in the dargah . . . a devotion that by turns energizes, elevates, makes you a part of the congregation and yet leaves you introspective and alone. Most critically of course, it is not the inanimate objects in the shrine that rivet your attention as they do in the mausoleums of kings and queens; in a Sufi shrine it is the living, pulsating life that surrounds the zinda pir that animates interest and emotion.

And yet, not all Sufi shrines are equally popular centres of veneration. In seeking to understand why and how some Sufi shrines developed and not others, I have studied two relatively unknown shrines with contrasting histories that are in close proximity to each other. The first is the shrine of Khwaja Maqbul Shah in the suburb of Saket and the second is the shrine of Sayyid Jalal al-Din Chishti in the adjoining Jahanpanah forest, less than a kilometre away. The architectural features of the first clarify that it is an old shrine, perhaps from the fifteenth-sixteenth century. The second shrine is relatively new, emerging as a site of veneration only in the 1980s. Despite their difference in age, it is the older of the two shrines that has declined into anonymity, its sacred character usurped by other elements. By contrast the shrine of Jalal al-Din Chishti has developed into a bustling pilgrimage centre. In studying these two relatively unknown shrines, I thought it useful to preface my narrative with a brief note on the shrine of Qutb al-Din Bakhtiyar Kaki (AD 1235) which is far better known. This shrine is also in South Delhi and it will help in contextualizing my account of the Saket and Jahanpanah shrines somewhat more clearly.

Sufism and the Shrine of Qutb al-Din Bakhtiyar Kaki

At first sight it may seem that some of the more abstract ideas in Sufism have little connection with the worship of saints. For example, self-abnegation is important in Sufism as is careful discipline and above all, a love of God that obliterates all other reality leaving the seeker, in turn, exalted at the prospect of close proximity with his beloved and sombre at the termination of that momentary ecstatic bliss. In its rejection of the material world and its transitory, external attractions, Sufism emphasized an intuitive insight into the inner hidden meaning of the revealed Word. In their search for spiritual truth, Sufis did not deny the relevance of the theological and juridical traditions of scholastic Islam.

Certainly God's Word, the Qur'an, was the usual point of departure in their search for an inner, ultimate reality. And yet, rather than simply adhering to a system of rituals and beliefs, Sufis focused upon the intention that rituals served, foregrounding the inner, esoteric meaning in God's revelation accessible only to spiritual adepts.

Very rarely God bestowed a special grace (barakat) upon select individuals, his friends (auliya), which allowed them the ability to comprehend this inner reality. For the larger part, however, some Muslims could hope to be guided to this truth through their spiritual preceptor, a pir/*shaykh*. Those who wanted to learn and follow the mystic path became *murids* or students of their teacher and lived in his hospice; others visited the master from time to time, listened to his sermons and remained a part of a lay congregation. Over time, a method of spiritual and mystical training developed within these fraternities, a method or a school (*tariqa*) that was passed down from one generation of teachers to the next, creating a venerable genealogy of masters (*silsila*). Whereas there were general philosophical similarities amongst these mystical schools they also differed sufficiently in key details and certainly in rituals, to distinguish one tariqa from another.

The Sufi shaykh Qutb al-Din Bakhtiyar Kaki belonged to the Chishti mystical tradition whose founders were collectively called the Khwajagan-i Chisht, the masters of Chisht, a small town in Afghanistan, just east of Herat. The individual who brought the Chishti tariqa to India was Mu'in al-Din Chishti who lived in Ajmer. He was followed by Qutb al-Din Bakhtiyar Kaki, Baba Farid Ganj-i Shakar and Nizam al-Din Auliya who established their respective hospices (*khanqahs*) in Delhi, Ajudhan in the Punjab and then in Delhi again. After the death of these shaykhs their grave sites emerged as important dargahs of pilgrimage; to the large number of people who cherished the barakat of these saints, their grace continued to emanate from their place of repose—they were all zinda pir.

There is little in the early Chishti records or in the early

Sultanate court chronicles that suggest the presence of a large body of disciples around Bakhtiyar Kaki or the emergence of his grave site as a mazar. And yet by the 1330s the Moroccan traveller to India, Ibn Batuta, mentioned that his grave was already a pilgrimage centre. From the sixteenth century, Bakhtiyar Kaki's shrine started receiving further subventions from the state. Inscriptions and extant construction in the shrine premises suggest that this started from the reign of Sher Shah Suri (1540-45), but declined somewhat between the reigns of Akbar and Shah Jahan, to pick up again from the years of Aurangzeb's rule into the mid-nineteenth century.[1] The ebb and flow in the popularity of Bakhtiyar Kaki's shrine was in part a consequence of the increasing attention paid to other Chishti centres like Mu'in al-Din's shrine in Ajmer, Salim Chishti's in Fatehpur Sikri and Nizam al-Din Auliya's in Delhi. But it was also reflective of the changes that occurred in the fortunes of the Chishti tariqa in the subcontinent. After its great popularity in the fourteenth–sixteenth centuries it was marginalized in the seventeenth by the increasing prominence of the Naqshabandi and Qadiri Sufi tariqas within courtly circles. It was with the beginning of the eighteenth century that the fortunes of Chishti mystics revived in Delhi and much of this coincided with increasing literary production that created a mystical halo around its chief proponents: Mu'in al-Din Chishti and Nizam al-Din Auliya.

The history of Bakhtiyar Kaki's shrine reflected the changing fortunes of the Chishti tariqa but the modern visitor might well miss this aspect of the dargah's history. Through the centuries the shrine witnessed hectic construction activity until it is impossible to trace any vestige of its original thirteenth century character. Perhaps the most obtrusive architectural element in the dargah would be the large number of tombs that litter the shrine. Contemporaneous with Bakhtiyar Kaki's tomb is the grave of the Suhrawardy saint, the famous Qazi Hamid al-Din Nagauri, a close friend and companion of Bakhtiyar Kaki. In consonance with the great reputation of Bakhtiyar Kaki's shrine in the eighteenth century, many post-Aurangzeb Mughal emperors chose to be buried in the precincts of his shrine. The graves of Shah 'Alam Bahadur Shah (1707–12), Jalal al-Din Shah 'Alam (1760–1806) and Mu'in al-Din Akbar (1806–1837) are in the close vicinity of the dargah of Bakhtiyar Kaki. The wish of the last Mughal ruler, Bahadur Shah 'Zafar' (1837–58) to be buried there as well was denied by the British.

Since Bakhtiyar Kaki was amongst the 'friends of God' (auliya) the great Sufi Shaykh would intercede with Him on behalf of his disciples at the day of judgement. That is why so many of them chose to be buried in his proximity. Bakhtiyar Kaki had prescient knowledge of how the hallowed spot would develop in the future. He was entranced by the area and stopped there, remarking on the 'aroma of hearts, *bu-yi dilha'* that suffused the area. Nizam al-Din Auliya, who had narrated this story, reminded his audience: 'See all the great nobles asleep there!'

The central feature of the shrine is, of course, the earthen grave of Bakhtiyar Kaki. This is covered with a chadar, because in Sufi cosmology the friend of God becomes the 'bride of Allah' upon his death. The chadar is then the pir's bridal veil and his death anniversary is celebrated annually as his wedding day or urs. Bakhtiyar Kaki did not want any structure over his grave and in deference to his wishes it remains covered with earth. Sometime in the eighteenth century, perhaps later, a cupola on the lines of Mughal balustrade columns was raised over it. Eventually glass pieces were embedded in it. Although the decor no longer matches Bakhtiyar Kaki's intentions, the decorations are not offensive. They add to the magical touch of the shrine making it gleam like a jewel.

There is peace and quiet in the precincts of the shrine. And also a fair bit of irony. We do not know Bakhtiyar Kaki's own sentiments on the subject but today no women are allowed in the sacred courtyard of the shrine. They are forced to worship from a distant corridor with a marble screen distancing them from their shaykh. Their entreaties to the shaykh are evident in the coloured strings tied to the marble screen, but the 'bride of Allah' remains distant and, quite paradoxically, accessible only to the male pilgrims. It is hard to say when this gender restriction started but it is noticeable in many—but not all—of the important Chishti shrines today.

An equally interesting structure, also relatively new in construction, is the *naubat khana*, the space occupied by musicians who would sing poems in praise of Allah's beauty, His mercy, and celebrate the life of His favourite, Qutb al-Din. In Sufism, this invocatory singing was described as *sama,* known today as qawwali. It was originally carried out under the strict supervision of the pir and Bakhtiyar Kaki often participated in it himself. In Qutb al-Din's shrine the original naubat khana was by the gate to the shrine and the open courtyard in its vicinity is still used by qawwals as a place to hold their assemblies. The more recent construction is within the shrine complex itself, not far from the mosque.

This might appear as an unusual place to hold sama gatherings because the mosque is a place of solemn, undisturbed worship. Sufi veneration of the Qur'an, the Prophet and his traditions, was second to none; they differed from learned scholars insofar as they were guided by their 'inner-light' (*nur-i batin*) in their interpretation of the holy texts. As a result a mosque had to be more than just a place where ritual was meaninglessly followed. Nizam al-Din Auliya explained the difference: 'Scholars are like children who are dragged to school to learn their alphabets. They manage to learn their *alif, be, pe* but they can never grasp the true meaning of these letters.'

Reading namaz was an integral part of Chishti practice and all their pirs discoursed at length on the efficacy of prayer, not just as a part of an obligatory exercise required of all Muslims, but because prayer and the recitation of specific verses from the Qur'an had miraculous consequences— they healed, consoled, and redressed difficulties. The presence of a mosque in Bakhtiyar Kaki's shrine was therefore not surprising, nor the fact that it was near the naubat khana.

But to perform the rituals of prayer it was necessary to provide a space for Muslims to perform their ablutions, *wuzu*, without which namaz could not be read. Some of the great mosques in the country have beautiful tanks in their central courtyards for this purpose and the shrine of Bakhtiyar Kaki outmatched any of these. It had a beautiful stepped well (*baoli*) very close to the mosque. The extant one was perhaps constructed in 1846 but it is unclear if this was new or replaced an older one on the same site. At any rate there is no sign now of the earliest source of water to the shrine and the baoli is full of debris and quite useless for the performance of wuzu. The shrine administrators have made a brand new arrangement with piped water for worshippers to perform their ritual ablutions. To be able to minister to the large number of pilgrims that arrived at Bakhtiyar Kaki's shrine they have also tried to make provisions for their welfare. The shrine has a soup-kitchen (*langar khana*) and a hospice (*jama'at khana*) for their food and overnight stay. These are new structures and while they may have had medieval antecedents, no trace of those are in evidence today.

The old and the new sit cheek by jowl within the dargah. Certainly post-Partition events have left a huge impression on the shrine. The old Muslim inhabitants of the village of Mehrauli, where the dargah was located, fled to Pakistan or to the city of Shahjahanabad as communal riots gripped the area. Their domiciles were taken over by émigrés from Pakistan and within a short period the social demography of the region altered. The Muslim population of the village declined and was replaced by new residents who were Hindus or Sikhs displaced from Pakistan; these people did not revere Bakhtiyar Kaki at all. As a result the shrine, once venerated by the last of the Mughals, was suddenly decontextualized from the social world of the population residing in its immediate vicinity. But its memory was never quite erased. The circulation of Chishti mystical records still kept its significance alive and even if it lacked local importance, pilgrims from distant regions still arrived in its precincts. The

Government of India also intervened to introduce secular rituals that were once associated with the shrine during the period of the Mughals. In the nineteenth century, during the fair of the flower sellers, the Sair-i Gul Firoshan, a procession would make its way through Mehrauli to the dargah of Bakhtiyar Kaki. It had lapsed during the turmoil of 1857 but was resurrected in the 1950s and is currently under the patronage of the Delhi government, and rechristened as the phool waalon ki sair, the procession of the flower sellers. It still makes its way through the village to Bakhtiyar Kaki's shrine *and* an old temple called Jog Maya.

Conservation groups often bemoan the loss of the original character of the shrine. Quite appropriately, they would like conservation and restoration work to protect the old, surviving medieval artefacts in the shrine. Unfortunately the antiquarian premise on which these recommendations are based ignores the fact that the old and the new are seamlessly conjoined within the precincts of the shrine. Since it is virtually impossible to separate the old from the new, it is also difficult to conserve selective parts of the shrine and not others. What we need to keep in mind are the sentiments of the pilgrims to Bakhtiyar Kaki's shrine for whom the credibility of the sacred centre comes from its lived character. This is not a static monument like the mausoleum of a dead ruler where squatters can be evicted and an attempt made to restore the structure to its authentic form. The shrine gains its meaning, instead, as the place of repose of a 'living' saint, 800 years old and still counting. Its basic elements, old and new, separately and together, underline the spiritual character of the arena and help us comprehend the complex layers of beliefs that constitute Sufism and the belief in dargahs and zinda pirs.

But conservation questions apart, there is also the realm of the historian which is interested in studying process and change. Although fascinating, the records at hand hardly tell us anything about the constitution of belief at different moments in time or the composition of the diverse bodies of pilgrims who visited it. Not only are we unaware of the larger contextual history of the shrine but we are also ill informed about the servitors who administered it over the centuries, their backgrounds and internal politics. In other words the textual records relating to the shrine cumulatively affirm the charisma of Bakhtiyar Kaki; they do not provide a history of the fluctuating fortunes of the shrine or the circumstances that allowed for its survival against dire odds.

The history of the two other shrines that I would like to consider is not as rich as the dargah of Bakhtiyar Kaki, but what they lack in historical depth they make up in ethnographic detail. This helps us understand the fluctuating fortunes of grave shrines more clearly and sharpens the questions that we bring to uncritical medieval narratives and their accounts of an uninterrupted history of worship and prosperity surrounding resplendent grave shrines.

The Dargah of Khwaja Maqbul Shah in Saket

As you drive into the modern suburb of Saket in South Delhi today and negotiate your way through its choked traffic, it is almost impossible to imagine the area as it was in the 1970s: mustard fields, sparse tree coverage, a lonely road, no traffic or pedestrians, the distant chug-chug of a tube-well interspersed with the mooing of ambling cattle and the tinkle of their bells. Without electricity, night fell rapidly on the area and the glow of dispersed, solitary kerosene lamps, the sound of crickets in the echoing silence only accentuated the enveloping darkness and sense of loneliness.

On one of the two main roads entering Saket was a huge peepal tree; you noticed it before you espied the ruined wall of the mosque over which it towered. Other than its obvious age the mosque was unimpressive. It was what is called a *qanati masjid*, a kind common during the Lodi period in the fifteenth and sixteenth centuries. At their inception, qanati masjids might have been perambulatory tent-mosques; the term qanat meaning canvas or tent. In their sedentary, stone and mortar incarnations, these mosques were constructed on a small pedestal where the only significant feature was the western *qibla* wall. Sometimes, as in the mosque in Saket, the remnants of a small courtyard enclosed by low walls would still be visible. The Saket qanati masjid was approximately fifteen metres wide and twenty-five metres deep.

Only the archaeologically minded would notice these details, however. The few people who visited the ruined mosque precincts in the 1970s did not go there to read their prayers and certainly not out of any antiquarian delight. They went to visit a small brick shed with an asbestos roof within the courtyard of the mosque. Inside this unplastered shed was a grave with a green chadar. This was the grave of Khwaja Maqbul Shah. Some flowers were strewn on the chadar and stubs of incense sticks littered the head of the grave. When I first noticed the ruined mosque wall and grave in 1975, there was no placard identifying the grave nor was there anything immediately visible in the mosque area to stop someone like me, a rare passer-by, to investigate and take another look.

I was back in a relatively more urbanized Saket in 1983, this time as an unemployed graduate student in dire need of divine intervention to improve my job prospects. My wife and I were taken to the grave in the asbestos-roofed shed by my mother-in-law, a more devout soul than us, and we offered flowers and sweets at the grave. This was when I met Abdul Wali Shah, the servitor of the shrine.

Abdul Wali Shah lived in a cluster of huts together with his extended family adjacent to the mosque. He was an old man, perhaps in his late seventies and was simply called 'Baba' by all relatives and visitors. He would greet me, send one of his scampering grandchildren to fetch tea and we would sit and chat on one of the string-cots under the peepal tree.

'Chat' is perhaps too strong a word to describe our exchanges because Baba Wali Shah was quite inarticulate. He would talk, his sentences prefaced by a gargle, his thoughts would taper off and he would start sentences several times over, spit constantly, stop and smile suddenly as if his thoughts had miraculously beamed themselves into your head. 'Chatting' was a frustrating exercise if you were engaged, as

I was, in discovering the history of the saint buried in the shed. All I was told was that his name was Khwaja Maqbul Shah and that he belonged to the time of Sultan Mahmud of Ghazni, in the early eleventh century. As I later discovered, from all the pre-Mughal rulers, the Baba was only familiar with the name of Mahmud of Ghazni and he knew nothing else about this Sultan or his iconoclastic activities. Baba Wali Shah was more interested in underlining the fact that he was a direct descendant of Maqbul Shah and that I should visit the ruin just behind the mosque. Here I followed his direction and discovered the ruins of a wonderful baoli, hidden from the mosque but barely fifteen metres to its east.

Although it was also in ruins, the baoli was clearly much larger and grander in its architectural conceptualization than the mosque. It was placed in a North–South orientation with a wide bank of steps on the south leading down to the tank. Its walls were crumbling and its base was filled with debris and silt. There was enough of the wall and arches to confirm that it could be dated, like the mosque, to the fifteenth-sixteenth century Lodi period. I was delighted to discover the baoli because it confirmed the diligence with which water resources in the South Delhi plain had been harvested from the thirteenth through the sixteenth centuries. The baoli together with the Hauz-i Rani and the Satpula sluice gate dam on the Jahanpanah city wall, tapped the rivulet that overflowed from the 'King's reservoir', Hauz-i Sultani, otherwise known as Shamsi Talab today, just south of the Qutb, before it meandered north to join the Yamuna, beyond Nizamuddin and Humayun's tomb. In contrast to the frequent remarks about bad planning leading to a dearth of water in the Sultanate cities of Delhi, public authorities and local residents in the middle ages had invested considerable wealth in harvesting the considerable water discharge of the seasonal streams from the western hills of the Delhi plain. The baoli in the Maqbul Shah shrine was another evidence of this phenomenon.

I continued to visit Baba Wali Shah through the 1980s

during which time the first signs of change in the dargah precincts became visible. Although the quality of our conversations was still frustrating, I had shifted from my original investigative empirical mode to one that studied his interaction with visitors to the grave shrine. Through the decade the number and social background of the visitors to the dargah had altered. It had started with the arrival of some Afghan refugees in the Saket colony after the Soviet invasion. These refugees were in search of a mosque in the convenient vicinity of Saket and, like many others, they had also noticed the old qanati masjid. In the meantime, its premises had been swept clean and the qibla wall whitewashed. Slowly a small gathering of Muslims would read the Friday prayers every week here. Their presence also attracted Muslim residents from the Hauz Rani village and although it had its own small mosque a trickle also started coming to the qanati masjid. I did not know this at that time but many of these developments coincided with the takeover of the mosque by the Delhi Waqf Board in 1979. This organization funded the maintenance and administration of select Muslim religious centres in the Delhi region. They were the ones who had the qibla wall whitewashed.

None of these developments had displaced the position of Baba Wali Shah and his family as descendants and servitors of Maqbul Shah's shrine. In fact the arrival of a larger number of people at the mosque could have theoretically helped in revitalizing the dargah as well. Instead there was tension in the air. The visitors to the mosque often came and conversed with the Baba; more appropriately, *tried* to converse with him. His poor communication skills were underlined by the presence of a young man who, as the imam of the mosque, led its small congregation of worshippers into prayer. He was a self-confident young man, scrubbed and clean, always dressed in a spotless, starched kurta-pyjama, passionate and articulate with claims to being a *hafiz*, a person who had memorized the Qur'an. This young man was often present when people came to converse with the indolent, hukka chugging Baba. Baba Wali Shah was the butt of interminable teasing: 'Tell the visitors some grand stories about Maqbul Shah,' the imam would chortle, 'regale them with stories about how he made his cot fly and made the wall move.' These remarks would be followed by much back-slapping and sniggers amongst the imam's intimates. The poor Baba would clear his throat, spit and explode, 'Yes, it is true he had miraculous powers, he did all that.' But Wali Shah had no magical tales, no parables of epic proportions, nothing through which he could communicate Maqbul Shah's spiritual charisma to his audience. In his inability to touch an emotional chord with his visitors it was the zinda pir who hardly appeared alive; the Baba was losing the battle with the mosque and its imam. It was not a scene that I enjoyed and I stopped going to the shrine.

Although I stayed away for nearly a decade, I drove or walked by the mosque regularly and could notice how change was sweeping the place. There was, to begin with, rapid construction on the site of the mosque. Its qibla wall was encased in fresh plaster and then extended until it disappeared completely within a resplendent, high ceilinged cloister. A new towering entrance to the mosque with a large dome was in the process of being constructed and a large hoarding declared that the structure was the congregational mosque, Jama Masjid, of the dargah of Maqbul Chishti. Since the hoarding still identified the place as a dargah, I thought of the construction activity as largely cosmetic in character—but I could not have been more wrong.

I revisited the dargah with some students in 1998. In the interim Baba Wali Shah had passed away. His descendents still resided on the premises but their access to the mosque was blocked; they resided in small rooms outside its walls. I asked after the new servitor of the shrine and met with blank stares. Instead I was directed to the new imam of the mosque, Maulana Shihabuddin. This was not the entrepreneurial young man that I knew from my past visits. Maulana Shihabuddin was appointed by the Waqf Board and he refused to talk with me. I was directed instead to the head of the Muslim community of the Hauz Rani village, Pradhan Haji Muhammad Jathariya. The mosque was now under his jurisdiction. Nobody spoke of the zinda pir Khwaja Maqbul Shah anymore; the mosque had hegemonized the entire premises. Khwaja Maqbul Shah's name adorned the hoarding at the entrance to the mosque but inside, his presence was palpably absent.

Past tensions between the imam and the Baba, the scale and quality of the ongoing construction within the mosque precincts had portended these trends, but I was unprepared for their enormity. The grave of Khwaja Maqbul Shah received an honoured space within the cloister of the mosque. It was now renovated with screens and decorated tiles, but significantly it lacked a chadar, the sign that would declare that it was the resting place of a pir who was a bride of Allah. Without it Khwaja Maqbul Shah was stripped of his Sufi identity; the zinda pir had finally passed away. My old friend, Baba Wali Shah was also buried in the mosque with only the humbleness of the grave distinguishing him from his pir.

The mystical, magical character of the old shrine was slowly eroded and each piece of stone and mortar consolidated the new scholastic, ritualistic incarnation of Islam within its premises. A school, *madrasa*, for young children was constructed on the side of the mosque and in the afternoons you would find young children in their ubiquitous kurta-pyjamas and skull-caps hunched over their slates, chanting rhythmically, swaying back and forth, trying to memorize their texts. The biggest shock occurred when I went to search for the baoli. It had vanished—completely disappeared! The huge stepped well was filled in with earth and only bits of forlorn wall on its south-east edge remained of the old grand structure. Descendants of Baba Wali Shah who had rooms not far away from this area, informed me of the Pradhan's plans to build a large madrasa for Qur'an instruction. There was no sorrow in their voices, only an excitement at the prospect of change and progress: an old ruin, which only accumulated garbage, had given way—what new, flamboyant building would come up in its stead?

It was not just the architectural environment that had altered in the dargah, the mood of the people and the reasons why they visited it had also changed. Whereas in the past my religious identity was not a subject of concern to anyone in the dargah, the new mosque and its administrators were extremely conscious that this was a space within which Islam was taught and reproduced. It had to be protected from a variety of different threats—and I was one of them.

This was the 1990s, the Babri masjid and the Bombay riots were not distant memories. Even more immediate were developments closer to home: the 'usurpation' of the common-lands of the Hauz Rani villagers by the DDA Saket Sports Complex, the resplendent renovation of a Sanathan Dharma temple down the street from the mosque, a renovation that had the support of the local residents' associations who prevailed upon city authorities to rename Saket's main street 'Mandir Marg'. The sense of being besieged was complete when the Marriott, Saket's lone five-star hotel, arrived as the immediate neighbour of the mosque and construction of the city's largest shopping mall commenced in earnest just behind the old baoli. If the Baba's fanciful stories carried the threat of lulling the faithful into believing in the miraculous power of saints and their supernatural abilities to intervene in the lives of disciples, the hotel and the mall were the devil's attempts at tempting Muslims into immoral consumption and promiscuous lifestyles. The new mosque was the bastion of Islam that protected the community from the influence of these pernicious ideologies. Haji Muhammad Jathariya, the Pradhan who had managed the mosque from its early construction years, guarded his achievements very jealously. He enforced strict discipline within the mosque precincts—comportment and speech were policed, conservative dress and gender discrimination were enforced. A heathen such as I, with a troop of young students—young adults of both genders, casually dressed and obviously having a good time in each other's company—spelled trouble. I was accosted, harangued and shooed away. The mosque was for Muslims, we were told, and we had no business there.

This was a conservative, defensive, ghettoized face of Islam familiar to the students thanks to the media coverage after 9/11. The students had not witnessed the other traditions of Islam that had occupied the same site just over a decade ago or had any knowledge of the historical interventions and debates that had led to the eventual success of the present version. Narrating its past was therefore important to provide the present with some context and to disturb the many stereotypes that they carried about Islam.

But the unfolding history of Khwaja Maqbul Shah's mosque has a final bittersweet twist to it. As it happened, Pradhan Haji Muhammad Jathariya died in 2006 and when I visited the mosque in 2007 no successor had as yet been appointed as a replacement. The hiatus, however, opened possibilities of discourse absent earlier. I had arrived there with the usual retinue of students but this time no one harangued us and the swarm of curious kids from the madrasa who surrounded us were shooed away. In fact, I had a very cordial conversation with a butcher who went so far as to advise me to ignore the maulvis if they were to harass us. 'The mosque,' he said, 'is a place of worship to God and everyone who comes here with respect is welcome.' The butcher had a shop in Saket and did not look at the expanding commercial opportunities in the neighbourhood with the abhorrence characteristic of the Haji. Without jeopardizing the dignity of his religion he gestured to future developments in the mosque precincts that saw in the consumerist evolution of Saket possibilities of profit, not threat. Times had changed and with it the dargah under the peepal tree had given way to a resplendent mosque that provided a different face of Islam to the residents and visitors to Saket.

The Shrine of Jalal al-Din Chishti Auliya in the Jahanpanah Forest

Less than a kilometre from Saket is a long, narrow stretch of greenery nearly five kilometres long, which starts at the village of Chiragh Dilli and curves towards the medieval fort of Tughluqabad. This is the Jahanpanah forest park with picnic areas interspersed with large idyllic wooded sections. I was bicycling through the forest with my daughter on a winter evening in 1984 when we chanced upon a grave-shrine. I was informed subsequently that this was the shrine of Jalal al-Din Chishti Auliya.

Quite in contrast to the shrine of Khwaja Maqbul Shah, this was clearly not a shrine of any antiquity. All it consisted of was a grave whose features were shrouded by a chadar. The grave rested on a recently constructed platform with an asbestos roof supported by concrete pillars. The chadar covering the grave was a heavy fabric, bright green in colour with sequin embroidery at the edges. Over the grave was an awning of the same colour as the chadar but of a lighter material and much richer in its ornamentation. Streamers hung from the awning and the asbestos roof as did stars and translucent paper globes in which oil lamps could be lit at night. The bright decorations and the awning attracted the gaze of visitors to the shrine giving it the appearance of a shining jewel in the midst of wild greenery.

A serious, devout looking man sat at the foot of the grave. He introduced himself as Muhammad Yaqub Chishti, the servitor (sajjada nishin) of the shrine of Jalal al-Din Chishti Auliya. As far as I could make out the tomb did not have a gravestone and I asked him how he knew that Jalal al-Din was buried here and what he knew about the saint. Yaqub told me that Jalal al-Din was an Auliya, a friend of God, who had lived centuries ago. He had appeared to Yaqub in a dream and directed him to his grave. Yaqub was instructed to clean the site and make it a place of pilgrimage. The zinda pir was awakening from his slumber and calling his disciples to him.

Quite in contrast to Baba Wali Shah, Yaqub was a born storyteller. He explained how his dream was like watching a show on television, a slowly unfolding story of Jalal al-Din's life and identification of his family members. They were all buried in the vicinity of the pir's tomb: 'His brother is buried under the tree over there, the grave of another is under the bush . . . they are all here, keeping Auliya sahib company.' I asked if Yaqub had any explanation why Jalal al-Din Chishti might have chosen him as his deputy. Yaqub suggested it must be because he was a distant descendant; the two did share the same last name—Chishti. This surname evoked powerful sentiments within Muslim circles in north India, referring as it did to the great spiritual lineage founded by Mu'in al-Chishti at Ajmer. This was a resplendent lineage to tap into and it was reflective of Yaqub's general facility at making a lingering impression.

Yaqub's demeanour, for example, was always kind, in an avuncular, contemplative and serious kind of way. He did not try to appear as your friend, but as a reflective guide with whom you could share your problems. Nor did he have long conversations with pilgrims. He listened attentively, summarized their grievances effectively and had quick, decisive solutions to offer. He did not ignore anyone, nor did he linger in his ministration over them. He was solicitous of women and their problems, always very correct and behaved like a condescending patriarch. On Fridays, he would give a brief sermon which would concern itself with general material problems faced by his audience—rising prices, difficulties in managing family budgets, inter-personal conflicts within the household—and would provide resolutions that would paraphrase the teachings of Jalal al-Din Chishti Auliya. The grace of the saint touched the audience through his servitor and the audience was always still and attentive as they listened to his discourse. This was important because only Yaqub was privy to Jalal al-Din's teachings which had appeared in his dreams. Pilgrims, should they have wanted, did not have recourse to any text.

Yaqub had ambitions for the dargah and his ministry. Although only recently summoned by his pir, he was completely pledged to his calling. He would personally sweep the pedestal of the grave and water the earth around the shrine twice a day. He planned on starting the urs celebrations in the near future with qawwali and food offerings. And eventually he planned to publish a compilation of the pir's teachings. Much as the imam had been in the Saket mosque, it was the servitor of the Sufi shrine in the Jahanpanah forest that was the entrepreneur.

More than the rudimentary dargah, the shrine's natural environs attracted me back periodically. Within a couple of years one could notice the gradual appearance of the formal trappings of a Sufi shrine in the forest. An additional asbestos shelter was constructed to the west of the grave. Pilgrims could shelter from the elements as they conversed with their zinda pir. There was no formal mosque or qibla wall for the longest time but prayer carpets would be spread at the appropriate time for namaz. There was no water in the shrine so clay pots first appeared and eventually large prefabricated water tanks so that worshippers could perform their wuzu before prayer. Yaqub could be quite inventive. He stuck to his promise of starting the urs celebration (the death/marriage anniversary) of the saint. I remember in 1986, when the shrine was still receiving water in clay pots, Yaqub did not have the means to invite professional qawwals (singers) for the urs. He compromised and brought cassettes of qawwali music and the forest echoed with their serenades played off his small Sony three-in-one.

The people who visited the shrine were from the neighbouring colonies: Sheikh Sarai, Ambedkar Nagar, Govindpuri, all largely poor and lower middle-class colonies. Yaqub was quite blunt about the composition of his audience: 'It is the poor who are troubled and need sustenance,' he said, 'the value of true belief has not yet penetrated the rich residents of Saket and Masjid Moth.' Simple as the preparation for the urs might have been, there was no gainsaying the quality of emotion generated on the day. A woman from Sheikh Sarai dashed up to the grave in an agitated manner and started weeping and banging her head on the pedestal: 'Why have you deserted me Baba,' she wailed, before bursting into tears again. Yaqub remained impassive and still through the whole event and when I asked why he did not intervene, he explained that she was a diwani, lost in ecstasy and love, and should not be interfered with. Counselling could wait till she was sober.

I could never discover any details about Yaqub's background. He was always very conscious about his position and stature which did not brook intimacy. But what was amazing about his teaching and comportment was the ease with which he imported stock Sufi ideas into his discourse. Take dreams, for example, which were of such significance to him in his discovery of his pir's tomb. To a sceptic this would be a figment of his imagination, credible only, it might seem, to the exceptionally simple-minded. But in Sufism dreams are the means by which the subconscious guides the dreamer towards reality. There are countless stories in Sufi texts on how pirs warned their disciples of impending danger, of instructions that disciples received subliminally. Dreams were a part of the Sufi nur-i batin, the hidden knowledge that mystic novices had to actualize in their search for true knowledge. In the case of Yaqub, this intuitive capacity had been activated by his pir the moment he called him to his service. Yaqub was also sensible to the binarism in Sufism—the sense of ecstatic bliss that came when the faithful felt close to God/Reality and the sense of loss as withdrawal from that momentary union set in. It was sensitively apparent in his treatment of the diwani pilgrim demanding proximity with her pir. Finally, it was also apparent in the strong emphasis that Yaqub placed upon the formal ritual of daily prayer. To those uninitiated into Sufism, namaz rarely goes beyond the boundaries of standing witness to the unity of God, acknowledging that all believers belong to one community equal in the eyes of their Maker, and submitting to His Word and final judgement. But the Sufis who find hidden meanings in the Qur'an also discover in the act of praying a powerful, enabling moment when they could gain proximity to God, absolve themselves of sin, gain favour and, depending upon their choice of chapter and verse, a remedy for specific afflictions. As we have already noticed, Sufi shrines, big or small, had a mosque on their premises where the faithful could read their prayers. Yaqub had not missed the significance of this ritual and right from the very beginning he tried to ensure that Jalal al-Din's shrine had provisions for the reading of namaz.

It would be some years before all of this could be put into place—and not all of it happened in Yaqub's lifetime. He passed away prematurely, I am not sure when exactly, because I did not visit the shrine through the 1990s. During the intervening period, however, I would drive by the Jahanpanah forest and notice signs of uninterrupted prosperity in the dargah: large hoardings had started appearing, advertising the shrine and the annual urs event.

Yaqub's ambitions for the shrine were coming true. After his death, his young son Muhammad Irfan became the next servitor of the shrine. He was every bit as efficient and impressive as his father. When I went back in 2005 it was during Ramazan. A huge congregation had gathered at the shrine in the evening. After circumambulating Jalal al-Din Chishti's grave, his disciples gathered at the small mosque where a decade ago Yaqub had spread prayer mats for namaz. After prayer all the worshippers partook in a community meal and broke their fast. Very graciously and without any reservation whatsoever they invited me to join them in a meal of pulao and curds.

In 2007, I visited the shrine again a day after the urs celebration. Although the festivities were over, streamers still decorated the entry to the dargah and it carried an expansive, festive air. They had live qawwali now. The central shrine now had a dome with Qur'anic verses inscribed on it. Verandas extended out from the grave shrine on all sides but it was still not large enough to hold the crowd of diverse people coming from distant areas and not just Delhi. Their clothes and deportment suggested their mixed social backgrounds; these were not all poor or lower middle-class pilgrims. I tried to take a photograph of the decorations inside the main hall. It inadvertently captured how the fervour of the urs celebration had not dissipated the day after the event: excitement was still in the air and the pushing and shoving of the crowd shook my camera. Despite all the changes the shrine was still a beautiful place, with twinkling lights encased in a green wilderness. Cats and dogs frolicked in its premises and nobody gave them another glance. As in Yaqub's lifetime it had made careful attempts to integrate with its habitat. The disciples would sprinkle flour mixed with sugar at the foot of the trees—for the ants or as an offering to the kinsmen of Jalal al-Din Chishti, I could not be sure.

Within twenty years, the father and son had turned an ordinary grave in the wilderness into a flourishing Sufi shrine. I marvelled at their management skills where prosperity and success was also related to their carefully calibrated reading of Sufism and scholastic Islam. As the shrine flourished and developed an institutionalized regimen the combination of these elements became somewhat more apparent. When I had talked with Yaqub in 1986 I had asked him whether his ministry at Jalal al-Din's grave had created any controversy—if he had faced opposition from anyone. I had deliberately left the question open-ended wondering if he would seize the opportunity to complain of the park administrators, the municipality or harassment from the local police constables. Yaqub did not rise to the bait. In fact, he made no reference to the civic administration of the city at all and spoke, instead, of the general hostility of the Deobandis towards Sufi shrines. Yaqub was alluding to the great educational institutions of religious learning at Deoband where jurisprudence, theology and grammar is imparted to aspiring scholars. In this institution a scriptural, textual version of Islam is taught and many of its graduates are the leading scholars, theologians and jurists in the subcontinent today. In their attempts to reform Islam they are often hostile and critical of what they regard as the superstitious innovations in practice amongst 'uneducated' Muslims. It was their ignorance, they believed, that promoted faith in amulets to ward off evil, miraculous stories of Sufi saints which deified mortals and created a false reliance on the efficacy of pilgrimage to Sufi shrines. Yaqub did not suggest that he was facing any direct hostility from these reformists but he gestured to their general criticism of Sufism and, since he now believed that he was an integral part of the mystical fraternity, he felt their challenge to his ministry as well.

As a part of a larger mystical fraternity, Yaqub and his son mimed the code of conduct of some of the more famous dargahs of Bakhtiyar Kaki and Nizam al-Din Auliya in Delhi. Not the least of these included the introduction of careful gender policing. In 2007, the excesses of a diwani pilgrim would not be tolerated within the dargah any longer. In fact, the sacred enclosure of the grave was declared out of bounds for women. Instructions on a pillar and the stairs declared that women were prohibited from going up to visit the pir's grave and instructions on an adjoining pillar reminded others to cover their heads. Here Yaqub's son did not depart from his father's vision; he seemed to only extend it. As the reach and influence of Jalal al-Din's shrine expanded and larger amounts of funds diversified the activities within the dargah, an effort was made to consolidate its position by integrating aspects of a juridically inspired version of Islam. The newly constructed mosque in the dargah also started doubling as a madrasa where Muslims families were invited to send their children to learn to read the Qur'an. Catechism in the details of the Holy Book did not contradict belief in the Sufi saint whose grace suffused the shrine. Instead, knowledge of the Qur'an only protected the believer from innovations and made him into a more accomplished Sufi. While diversifying its role in the lives of the local Muslim community, the presence of the madrasa in the shrine also helped in taking the edge off any hostile criticism from reformers like the Deobandis and Barelavis.

Within a couple of decades and without any claim to antiquity, land and subventions from the Waqf Board, the dargah of Jalal al-Din Chishti Auliya had gained enough importance to be listed on an internet website as one of Delhi's important Sufi shrines (http://www.aulia-e-hind.com/dargah/delhi.htm#13). Whereas the shrine of Khwaja Maqbul Shah with all of its potentially viable historical claims disappeared within the renovated Jama Masjid, the zinda pir Jalal al-Din Chishti arose from his repose in the woods of Jahanpanah and through the efforts of his servant, Muhammad Yaqub Chishti, emerged as the dispenser of succour and protection amongst his disciples.

Conclusion

As we review the account of the three Sufi shrines discussed in this paper one of the interesting subjects that we could contrast would be the source(s) of information available to the student of these shrines. In the case of the Saket and Jahanpanah shrines there are no textual records at all and we have to rely primarily on the history provided to us by the servitors of the two shrines, the accounts of other protagonists and visitors and our own observations. All these materials are also available for a study of the shrine of Qutb al-Din Bakhtiyar Kaki, but we also have access to additional textual records of some antiquity. These are either Sufi texts or a variety of epigraphs. Historians, who read these accounts, process them in ways very different from the oral accounts of the servitors in the Saket and Jahanpanah shrines. There is a suspension of disbelief as we read Nizam al-Din Auliya's fourteenth century anecdotes about Bakhtiyar Kaki's life. We respectfully accept the sentiments regarding the grace of the Sufi pir present in these accounts, partly because they are old, partly because they are textual and partly because they confirm our pre-existing assumptions about the greatness of the saint buried in its precincts. We should not miss the circularity in our thought processes here where a critical examination of Qutb al-Din's shrine falters under the baggage of our a priori assumptions of his greatness. Although the historical records concerning Qutb al-Din's shrine function much like Yaqub's presentation that extolled Jalal al-Din Chishti's charisma, we display greater scepticism in accepting Yaqub's account because it is without textual corroboration, its oral character further prejudiced by its presentist character. In the absence of the trappings of history to support his claims, Yaqub is regarded as an entrepreneur 'manipulating' Sufi sentiments for profit. By contrast Bakhtiyar Kaki's reputation as a great, devout Sufi saint remains untarnished. Following this mode of interpretation, the success and failure of a shrine in retaining its popularity over the long duration is regarded as a reflection of the pietistic stature of the pir—the older the flourishing shrine the more 'authentic' the attributes of its saint. In this context, Bakhtiyar Kaki emerges as a far greater saint than the recently discovered Jalal al-Din and Maqbul Shah whose congregation frittered away.

Without our being conscious of it, our mode of analysis of the 'great' shaykhs and their dargahs is trapped in the didactic content of our sources. Rather than the individual stature of saints, whether they were 'great' or not, the example of the Saket and Jahanpanah shrines guides us towards a different body of questions that we could foreground in our study of centuries old shrines like Bakhtiyar Kaki. These would demand a more careful study of sources: what metaphors of belief and faith, what technologies of mobilization were harnessed to attract followers and pilgrims to shrines? Since shrines like Bakhtiyar Kaki's are of considerable antiquity, surely the historical contexts and the participants themselves altered significantly over the distance of four centuries? The vocabulary of faith used to articulate belief in the grace of the zinda pir reflects both, the changes that have occurred in the contexts of the shrine and a synchronic adherence to central ideas of Sufism. It is interesting to unravel this change and continuity, the dialectics between the past and the present, not just so that we can comprehend the history of Sufism more precisely but also the ways in which our own individual identities and ideologies are constituted.

From a slightly different perspective, we also need to remain sensitive to the mixed feelings that can be provoked by the transformations and contrasting histories of the three Sufi shrines in South Delhi. There is certainly the sense of a huge loss as the character of Khwaja Maqbul Shah's dargah altered into the renovated Jama Masjid and the old baoli was completely destroyed. A sixteenth century shrine had whimpered to an end, its mystical magic replaced with the stone and mortar of a doctrinal Islam that appeared unbending and intrusive. The loss of a time of innocence and its replacement by shrewd market forces also seemed to play out in the Jahanpanah forest where, some would argue, an entrepreneur converted an anonymous grave into a flourishing Sufi shrine. The making of the shrine altered the fortunes of its sajjada nishin, a seemingly cynical deployment of mysticism and market forces that appeared to be in consonance with the rampant consumerism in the area.

And yet beyond this sense of loss there were larger structural features about these developments which should make us pause and reflect about the constitution of Islam. The shrine of Jalal al-Din Chishti and the Jama Masjid of Khwaja Maqbul Shah in Saket emerged, in their own ways, as extremely venerable and successful centres of Islam where their respective congregations were socialized into related but contrasting versions of Islam. Rather than studying them as discrete entities, they need to be studied within a larger dialectical frame of reference sharing a common spatial and intellectual topography. The triumph of scholastic Islam in the Saket Jama Masjid and of Sufism in the Jahanpanah shrine are reflective of how the multiple strands of Islam continue to flourish and gain adherents within a kilometre of each other. It is the vibrant success of these alterities, each of them deriving their meaning from integral aspects of Islam that mark the Muslim community's resistance to efforts at homogenization. In this we should never understate the challenges that they have to face from both, endogenous as well as exogenous forces. And as long as these multiplicities continue to flourish in their proximate habitats, Islam and Muslims will remain in (contentious) dialogue with the great traditions that constituted them over time. A study of the textual materials relating to the shrine of Bakhtiyar Kaki can very usefully bring out the nature of this dialectic over the long duration.

Because of the ways in which the world is polarized today it is actually quite easy to ignore this diversity and debate. We forget that it is the most dogmatic, literalist, militant forms of the Muslim tradition that are frequently represented as *the* true face of Islam. It is the rhetoric of this representation that frames our current understanding of Islam and its relationship with the world. Attempts to challenge these representations have often led to the cry of 'Islam in danger'—a danger that is formulated as much from exogenous neo-colonial forces as it is from endogenous militant fundamentalist groups. But it is important to point out that the fears for Islam's future are articulated only when there is an inability to notice and appreciate its divergent practices, assuming for the moment that individuals like the Pradhan Haji Muhammad Jathariya or the servitor of the Jahanpanah shrine, Muhammad Yaqub Chishti, alone, speak for the religion. And yet neither of these venerable masters nor their congregations comprises the 'church' of Islam. Since our imagination is sometimes constrained and quite unable to conceive the larger, diverse and amorphous character of the Muslim community, a momentary reflection on the two Sufi shrines in South Delhi helps in bringing into focus the contrasting histories that lend form and substance to the faces of Islam and being a Muslim today. Beyond the simple sadness that one feels at the course of events that led to loss of the dargah of Maqbul Shah, we should perhaps pay equal attention to the flourishing, newly constructed Saket Jama Masjid and the pride and joy that it brings to those who pray in it. Concurrently (and *not* separately) we also need to look towards the equally prosperous Jahanpanah shrine of Jalal al-Din Chishti and its pilgrims. The presence of *both* stands as a heartening reassurance regarding the survival of multiplicities, debate, dissension and the politics of negotiation that determine [unpalatable perhaps to some of us, but still] free choices. We need to research, document and debate these multiplicities, not just to protect our heritage and enable informed choices for its future—but also to be aware of how it is this process of learning and remembering that keeps all of us in India and elsewhere, finally, out of danger.

Notes

1 For details on the construction see Maulvi Zafar Hasan, *Monuments of Delhi: Living Splendour of the Great Mughals and Others: Mehrauli Zail* (New Delhi, 1997; reprint of 1920 edition), 3:25–49. For an account of the shrine from the late Mughal period see Dargah Quli Khan, *Muraqqa'-i Dihli*, edited and translated into Urdu by Nurul Hasan Ansari (Delhi, 1982), pp. 23–25, 119–121.

Pradip Krishen

Avenue Trees in Lutyens' Delhi: How They Were Chosen

Have you ever wondered how particular kinds of trees were chosen to line the avenues of Imperial New Delhi? It's a curious list of trees in some ways, because British planners seem to have consciously avoided planting trees like the mango, shisham and banyan that were in vogue as avenue trees in northern India through Mughal times. Where did the ideas and inspiration come from?

There's a fair amount of information about New Delhi's avenue trees in the archival record. I found it revealing to poke around in the ashes, so to speak, and to make the kind of discovery that goes: 'Ah! So they didn't plant shisham because they didn't like its leaf litter', or 'They didn't want the piloo because it is associated with the graves of pirs', and so on. Here's the larger picture, deduced from the files and notings of horticulturists, architects, foresters and bureaucrats who all played a part in choosing and rejecting certain species.

Maps of New Delhi in 1938 show Lutyen's Delhi bounded by the river in the east, the Ridge (as negative space) on the west, the railway line near Safdarjang Aerodrome to the south, and the northern boundary showing roughly where Asaf Ali Road was later created.

Tree Scheme in Lutyen's Delhi

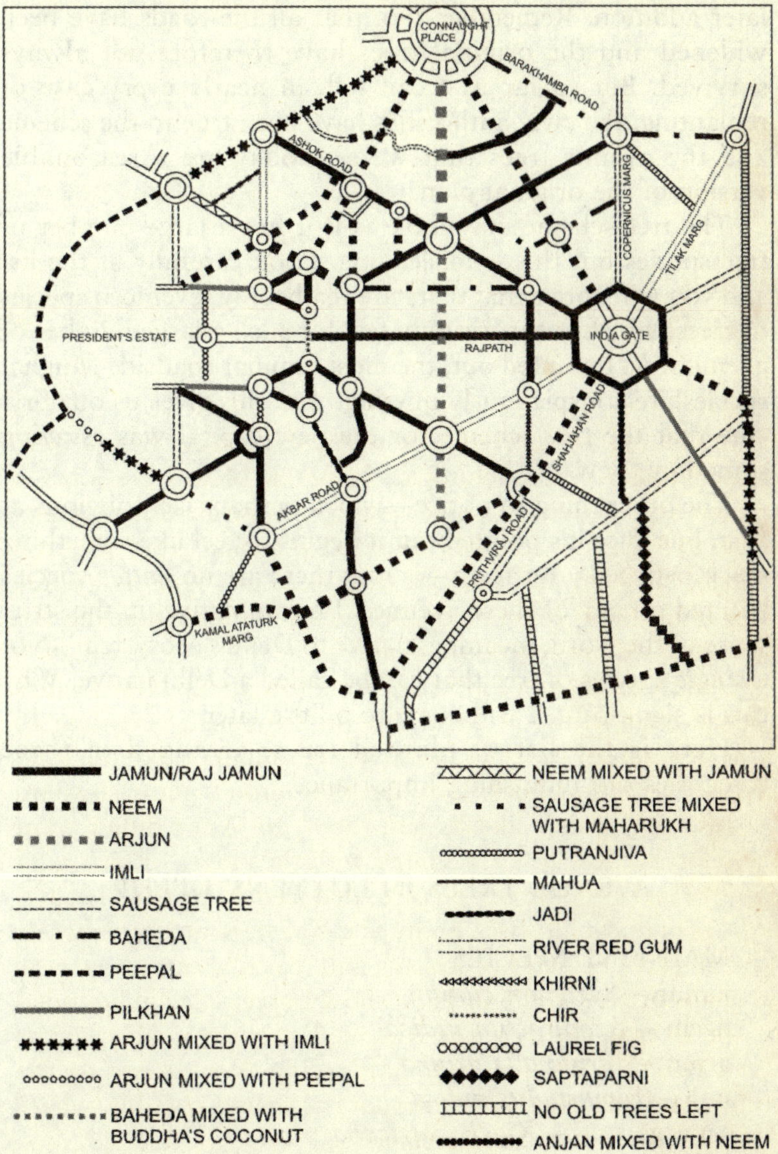

The map shows you the scheme of trees planted between 1913 and about 1935. Don't look for the amaltas, which forms a second line of trees on Akbar Road today, because it is a later addition. Remember too, that all the roads have been widened and the original trees have therefore not always survived. But so far as I can tell, in nearly every case of replanting, the civic authorities have been true to the scheme and the avenue trees that we see today are a reasonable version of the original plan.

The tree-scheme may look as if it has a large number of tree species but this is misleading. Look carefully at the list and you will notice that there are really only seventeen species of trees, which is surprisingly few for such a large number of avenues. As I pointed out, the most familiar roadside Mughal species are conspicuously missing. And this gives us our first clue that the tree scheme for the new capital was essaying something new.

The other thing to notice—which perhaps isn't obvious at first, but once it's pointed out it begins to feel like something stuck between your teeth—is that there are no *native* species planted on any of these avenues. I mean 'native' in the strict sense of the word, meaning 'native to Delhi's ecosystem'. Not a *single* species of tree that can be called a Delhi native. Why this is significant, I will come to a little later.

Here is the list of planted trees, arranged in three categories of diminishing importance:

AVENUE TREES IN LUTYENS' DELHI

MAINLINE SPECIES
jamun – *Syzigium cumini*
neem – *Azadirachta indica*
arjun – *Terminalia arjuna*
imli – *Tamarindus indica*
sausage tree – *Kigelia africana*
baheda – *Terminalia bellirica*

LESS COMMON SPECIES
peepal – *Ficus religiosa*
pilkhan – *Ficus virens*
putranjiva – *Drypetes roxburghii*
mahua – *Madhuca longifolia* var. *latifolia*
jadi – *Ficus amplissima*

RARE SPECIES – AND ONLY IN MIXED AVENUES
khirni – *Manilkara hexandra*
river red gum – *Eucalyptus camaldulensis*
maharukh – *Ailanthus excelsa*
buddha's coconut – *Pterygota alata*
anjan – *Hardwickia binata*
usba – *Ficus microcarpa*

When you peer closely at where the species were planted, it's abundantly clear that there are only six main species chosen as flagship trees that were stamped on a number of avenues, like handblocks. The jamun is probably the most common among them, planted along Tughlak Road, Rajaji Road, Tyagaraj Marg and a number of other roads.

The neem too is exceedingly common—you find it on Safdarjang Road, Prithviraj Road, Ashok Road, Tees January Marg and elsewhere.

The other mainline trees are the arjun, imli, sausage tree and baheda, which together with the jamun and neem make up a short-list that accounts for something like 85 per cent of the avenue trees in Lutyens' Delhi.

In a distinctly lower key are five species that were more sparingly used. The mahua for instance—that beautiful tree from the dry jungles of central India—was planted *only* along Southend Road (now Rajesh Pilot Marg) leading from Claridges Hotel to Lodi Garden. The peepal and pilkhan too were planted with noticeable restraint, almost as if the people who chose them were not quite sure if they were 'right' for the boulevards of an imperial capital.

And then, in another register, are six more tree species

which we can only regard as tentative experiments. I say this because they seem to have been planted with noticeable trepidation, tucked away in some inconspicuous, minor connective road or mixed in with another species. None of them are traditional avenue trees, at least not in northern India. The anjan, for example, is found in dry, volcanic soils in central India and grows into a large, magnificent tree in its natural habitat. But as far as I know, it had never been planted in a city before, certainly not north of the Deccan. The baheda is a magnificent, towering forest tree, but apart from a single instance in central India, it has not been planted along a street. It is difficult to avoid the impression that it was a case of planting these six species to see how they would do, before extending their provenance. These were trees on trial, as experiments.

For me, two things stand out in the tree list.

First, for an area this large, for the number of avenues that were available for planting (early in the twentieth century), this is a very small number of tree species. The planners could have chosen thirty or forty different species. They could have used a distinctive emblematic species for *each* major avenue. But the Imperial Capital Committee in its Report of 1913 says it has picked out thirteen species of trees out of a very large number of candidate species. And for us, peering back almost a century later, this is the surprising thing—why *only* thirteen species? (Somewhere along the way, the original scheme became muddied or diluted in some way, and the thirteen species grew to seventeen. That's still a very small number.)

*

The first clues to what was in store are in the *First Report of the Town Planning Committee for the New Imperial Capital in 1912-1913*. From our perspective the key person on the committee was its chairman, Capt. George Swinton, formerly chairman of the London County Council. In December 1912

Swinton drafted a *Preliminary Report on the New Capital Scheme* with a section called *Notes on Trees, Avenues and Various Other Details To Do With The Layout*

> In all countries there is a tendency to increase the number of trees and gardens in towns. In the European quarters of Indian cities this is no novelty, and undoubtedly, with us, in spite of the desire to mass the more important buildings for architectural effect, there will be few streets of houses, *trees will be everywhere, in every garden however small it be, and along the sides of every roadway, and Imperial Delhi will be in the main a sea of foliage. It may be called a city, but it is going to be quite different from any city that the world has known* . . . [emphasis mine]
> Naturally fine trees must be encouraged. In the reports on trees which have been prepared we find that the average height on maturity of most of the suitable trees is at least sixty feet. Of the fig tribe, the banyan, the pakar and the pipal, which are said to be the longest livers, are expected to grow to eighty feet. The mango is also eighty, the jaman and the tamarind seventy, and the nim sixty feet.

Trees were clearly terribly important to the intended effect. But why was Swinton so concerned with their *height*? He felt that since Delhi is mostly a flat plain, it is possible to have 'a monotonous green city just as easily as you can have a dull grey one', but also

> . . . to give relief of light and shade and prevent it from being as commonplace as the average cantonment, it is essential that there should be some outstanding features.

What *features* did Swinton have in mind? He urged that as far as possible all major avenues in New Delhi must be drawn so that they lead to vistas and showcase 'architectural effects' such as Indrapat (the old name for the Purana Qila), Safdarjang's Tomb, Government House (now Rashtrapati Bhavan), the Secretariat, the Lodi Tombs, and so on. One of the most significant sentences in the Report, from our point of view, is where Swinton says:

> . . . our real difficulty in New Delhi is not going to be to hide ugly things but to prevent what we want to be seen from being hidden . . .

The likely culprit? Trees, of course. Trees that grow too big. Trees wrongly chosen.

So from the beginning, before a single stick has been planted in the new capital, Swinton is saying, 'We want trees, of course, but there is a danger that they will become visual impediments, that they will grow too large and block off fine views, and therefore the choice of species, based on the height and spread to which they grow, is of crucial importance.'

Tucked away in the *Final Report of the Town Planning Committee* is a paragraph that shows how important this consideration was:

> . . . the size of the special trees selected for the avenues determine the width of avenues in which they are to stand. For the purpose of getting the right effect from the design of an avenue both the size and shape of trees are of importance; and with this end in view the Committee have (*sic*) picked out thirteen kinds of avenue trees out of a very large number, which will grow in Delhi . . . A deviation from the kind of tree selected to suit each avenue means a loss of a large general effect.

It is tempting to speculate on how this list might have been drawn up. There would almost certainly have been three or four categories of trees grouped according to their height and spread. It's a pity that I have not been able to lay my hands on this list, because nearly a century on, it might have raised a smile or two. Simply because trees often don't behave in the way planners expect them to, especially when they have been plucked out of a natural context and domesticated and arranged in straight lines in cities.

So how then were the actual trees selected? Who was it who would have known enough about candidate trees to have made up the initial lists? It's important to remember that the members of the Committee were not men who were likely to know very much about Indian trees, even though Swinton had spent time in India as ADC to a Viceroy and Lutyens enjoys something of a reputation for his gardens in England.

The *actual* business of deciding what to plant along the new avenues, still being planned, not yet built, would have begun some time before July 1912, when nurseries to house young trees intended for the avenues were set up—one in Mubarak Bagh (in north Delhi) and the other in the new Cantonment that was still being built near Palam. (There was also a small tree nursery set up in Isa Khan's Tomb, near Humayun's Tomb.)

From the archival record, it appears that the work and experience of two men, in particular, was crucial at this time. One was A.E.P. Griessen who spent many years in charge of the Taj Mahal gardens at Agra and was brought over to Delhi first to hurriedly tidy up the gardens and shrubberies of the Durbar Camp in 1911, and then was hand-picked to take charge of gardens and tree-planting in the new capital by Lord Hardinge himself. So Griessen was already in Delhi as Superintendent of Gardens at the time the Report was prepared.

The other key plantsman was R.H. Locke, 'European Gardener' in Delhi well before the new capital project was announced, and who stayed on as Superintendent, Government Gardens. (He later became 'Superintendent, Horticultural Operations in New Delhi'.)

The first list of trees that I found, referred to as 'Lutyens'

Selection', was almost certainly based on inputs provided by Griessen and Locke:

Lutyens' Selection	**(October 1912)**
jamun	*Syzigium cumini*
silky oak	*Grevillea robusta*
safed siras	*Albizia procera*
eucalyptus	*Eucalyptus tereticornis*
goolar	*Ficus racemosa*
wild date palm	*Phoenix sylvestris*
faraash	*Tamarix aphylla*
imli	*Tamarindus indica*
casuarina	*Casuarina equisetifolia*
toon	*Toona ciliata*
shisham	*Dalbergia sisso*
mango	*Mangifera indica*
neem	*Azadirachta indica*
maulshree	*Mimusops elengi*
khirni	*Manilkara hexandra*
ashok	*Polyalthia longifolia*
mahagony	*Swietenia macrophylla*
buddha's coconut	*Pterygota alata*

This is an interesting list for a few reasons: for one, it represents what is pretty much standard fare for the trees that were *already* being planted along city roads in north India early in the twentieth century. Mango, shisham, jamun, eucalyptus, neem, imli—these are all stock-in-trade city trees for that time. Entirely unsurprisingly, Lutyens had been provided with a *standard* tree list by the Delhi horticulture men. These were trees they were used to planting along city streets. Lutyens' list broke no new ground.

What is also interesting about the list is the trees that are *missing*. No arjun, for example. No peepal. No mahua, sausage tree, pilkhan, putranjiva . . . In the light of the tree scheme as we know it today, only three mainline trees—the jamun, neem and imli—figure in Lutyens' list. Along with two very minor ones—the khirni and Buddha's coconut.

Lutyens' list was clearly just the starting point of the exercise.

His list was then seen by the Viceroy, Lord Hardinge himself, who took a keen, personal interest in all aspects of the new Capital project because in many ways he saw it as a monument to his own viceroyalty. In the margin of the file, Hardinge wrote, 'Ask Mr Clutterbuck of the Forest Deptt to give his valuable advice and information on the subject.' Hardinge had described Peter Clutterbuck to Lutyens as 'about the most able forest officer in India'. His blue-eyed tree-man.

And so a telegram was sent from the imperial government to the provincial government of UP requisitioning Clutterbuck's services to prepare a report on 'the shady trees and ornamental shrubs that are likely to prosper in New Delhi'. Two months later, Clutterbuck finished his Report and neatly sidestepping the question of 'ornamental shrubs', made his case for what trees should be planted along the avenues of the new capital. It is this Report—in my opinion—which probably had the most influence on what trees were eventually chosen. Though as we shall see, even Clutterbuck's list does not give us the *exact* scheme as we know it today.

What trees did forester Clutterbuck like? We know precisely, because not only does he list the trees he approves of, he tells us what he likes about them. Furthermore, he critiques the trees in Lutyens' list and tells us which ones he thinks are no good and for what reasons.

Clutterbuck's first list was called 'Avenue Trees First Class'.

Avenue Trees First Class

imli	*Tamarindus indica*
ashok	*Polyalthia longifolia*
anjan	*Hardwickia binata*
rohini	*Soymida febrifuga*
maulshree	*Mimusops elengi*

arjun	*Terminalia arjuna*
banyan	*Ficus benghalensis*
pilkhan	*Ficus virens*
usba	*Ficus microcarpa*

It's a small, precise list, and once again if you compare it with the list of trees we know to be present today, it's remarkable for what's *not* there. But the arjun makes its appearance for the first time, and the anjan and usba too. It is difficult to avoid the impression that these were a forester's choices based on what he knew of these trees in their *natural* surroundings, because they were not common avenue trees at the time.

Clutterbuck presented thirteen more trees in 'Avenue Trees Second Class'.

Avenue Trees Second Class

jamun	*Syzigium cumini*
mango	*Mangifera indica*
muchkand	*Pterospermum acerifolium*
safed siras	*Albizia procera*
dillenia	*Dillenia indica*
gul mohur	*Delonix regia*
buddha's coconut	*Pterygota alata*
neem	*Azadirachta indica*
karanj	*Pongamia pinnata*
putranjiva	*Drypetes roxburghii*
camphor	*Cinnamomum camphora*
gaab	*Diospyros malabarica*
eucalyptus	*Eucalyptus tereticornis*

Here Clutterbuck includes the neem, mango, jamun and so on, but in each case he has some niggling reservations about them, which is why they have been relegated to the Second Class.

Clutterbuck wrinkles his nose about the neem and says: '. . . quite a weed in Delhi and too common for permanent avenues. It is quick growing and suitable for planting *temporarily.*' Of the mango he says: 'A fine tree giving cool shade. Handsome shiny foliage, very suitable for avenues, but is a very common tree.' About the jamun he says something similar: a fine tree, but much too common.

Clutterbuck then produced two more lists which he probably didn't expect anyone to take seriously because one is called 'Trees which are quick-growing but are leafless in cold weather or untidy'. The other is 'Trees with Bright Flowers but Leafless in the Cold Weather'. A bit like saying, 'Here are some of the other trees that are commonly planted but we don't *really* want any of these, do we?'

It is here in these negative lists that we begin to discover why the amaltas, siras, shisham, toon, jarul and the kachnars have all been left out of the Big Scheme. Their chief sin? *Being leafless in the cold weather.*

This is amplified in Clutterbuck's comments on the trees in Lutyens' List. He approves of the jamun, mango and maulshri as fine, good trees. The ashok? Excellent, he says, very handsome and *evergreen.* The imli, he says, is fine . . . a bit slow-growing, so you must plant things in front of it while it's growing up. The imli only just makes the grade as a suitable avenue tree.

Clutterbuck however says 'no' to neem, khirni, silky oak, shisham, faraash (*Tamarix aphylla*), mahogany, toon, casuarina, the wild date palm and the goolar. About the neem he is downright supercilious : 'Almost a weed', he calls it. 'Evergreen and quick growing. Suitable for temporary avenues with better slow-growing species behind to form the permanent avenues later on.' Clutterbuck wants the neems weeded out as soon as 'better' trees have grown up to take their place.

Here in a nutshell is the official process, with planners, gardeners, arboriculturists, foresters, all being asked to submit their lists and their reasoning. But remember that they are by no means the only people with opinions of what to plant.

Sir George Birdwood was a retired greybeard from the

Bombay provincial service who, around the time that New Delhi was being planned, busied himself in offering unsolicited advice to everyone who had anything to do with the project. In October 1913, with tree-planting plans still on the anvil, he wrote to Viceroy Hardinge:

> I have great experience of the planting of trees, and the Park-like Avenue (*i.e. Kingsway*) should be planted as soon as its alignments . . . have been accurately pegged out. The soil should be dug down six feet at least, and filled and left to settle, and then filled up again with the richest soil from the banks of the Ganges; and if those responsible on the spot desire, I would send Your Excellency a list of the great trees I know would flourish best there. I should especially include—*Erythrina indica*, scarlet; *Lagerstroemia flos-reginae*, purple, and *Poinciana regia*, scarlet and yellow.
> I believe I gave the name of 'Flos-Reginae' to the gigantic *Lagerstroemia* in honour of Queen Victoria, but I don't think the name has been adopted by Botanists . . . [*actually, they did. But the botanical name has since changed*]
> I should largely depend on trees with noble i.e. glossy evergreen leaves. And I would include all Indian trees sacred to Muslims and Hindus. As a matter of fact, the Viceroy should present a hundred plants each of *Crataeva religiosa*, the most sacred plant of the Muslims, and emblem of immortality to each great Muslim mausoleum within the Imperial radius of Delhi.

Here's another gem from 1932, a letter from Quarter Master General Wardrop to the Vicereine:

> Dear Lady Willingdon,
> Last night, at the Chief's, I ventured to make a suggestion to you about Delhi trees. Your Excellency

> told me to remind you of this and to give you the name of a certain tree.
>
> I suggest that the trees in New Delhi, along the sides of the roads and, here and there, in geometrical lines recall chiefly Wimbledon and Upper Tooting. Doubtless the reply would be that we are only copying the old Mogul ideas.
>
> Yet, I think a few small groups, clumps, of trees such as one sees in the park of any big English Estate . . . would add a graciousness now sadly lacking.
>
> If such should be planted, then they should certainly include numerous 'banyans'— those fine trees that drop their roots from their boughs. Calcutta, Cawnpore, Madras, Lahore have many such. I camped under one, when after tiger, that measured 390 yards in the circumference of its noon day shade . . .

Such gratuitous advice from people outside the horticultural establishment may sound faintly amusing to us but these are people who could not be taken lightly. If you track Wardrop's 'suggestion', it travels from Lady Willingdon's daak to the Viceroy's Military Secretary and from him to the President of the New Delhi Municipal Committee, who marks it to Russell and Mustoe who are by this time (1932) in charge of gardening and arboriculture in New Delhi.

Russell eventually wrote back to the President of the NDMC saying sorry, can't do it, banyans 'would be altogether too overpowering'. But even if it does sound colonial and quaint, it is useful to remember that this too was one of the ways that could lead to a certain tree being chosen. It didn't happen on this particular occasion. But what might have happened if Lady Willingdon had taken a fancy to a *Michelia champaca*, for instance, and said, 'Oh do let's have those darling little trees all along Roberts Road instead of those beastly, ugly ar-joons . . .'! I'm sure this sort of thing happens even now—in a different accent and tone, of course. But the point is that these voices do get heard, because they come from a great height.

*

In drawing up lists of candidate trees for the new capital city, two overriding criteria crop up again and again.

One is evergreen-ness. When gardeners or horticulturists are advocating the attributes of one tree or arguing against the selection of some other, they say, 'We don't want this species because it sheds its leaves and looks untidy'. Or more positively, 'We like this species because it is evergreen'.

Another value-loaded term plays its part. 'We don't want "common trees" is a repeated refrain in Clutterbuck's pronouncements. The neem? Too common, he says—almost a weed. Mango? Handsome, suitable for avenues, but far too common. Even the jamun is too commonplace to be eligible as a First Class Avenue tree. All these men who are pondering what to plant in New Delhi seem to be saying: we want these avenues to stand out, to be different, to be noticed. We don't want the new Imperial Capital city to look like another cantonment.

Together, these two factors explain—at least to my satisfaction—why the Tree Scheme for the new capital city was so different from Mughal schemes of avenue trees. And they probably go a long way towards explaining why there is not a single tree that is truly native to the Delhi region and its natural ecosystem. All of Delhi's native trees, after all—*every* single one—is deciduous.

What is it about *deciduousness* that these people found so undesirable?

If you think about it, most of the trees that we like in this city are leafy and green through April or May till long after the rains. And then just as we begin to crave some warm sunshine in December and January, these trees drop their leaves and let in the sun and that is the way we want it. Then when March and April come around, we get a wonderful spectacle of red or pink new leaves, or impossibly pale green leaves, which in many instances are every bit as beautiful as the fall colours that are celebrated in temperate climates.

So what is it about trees *that drop their leaves* that was so despised? So much so that deciduousness virtually became a disqualification for being planted on Delhi's avenues. Could it have been the leaf litter, the *practical* difficulties of keeping streets clean? Was it a value judgement by people who were used to severe, snowy winters, who didn't want to be reminded about those long, gloomy days when their trees remain bare—some kind of 'temperate reflex'? Was it perhaps something of an aesthetic judgement? Did it have to do with their stereotype of a tropical country—a hot, steamy country with green leafy trees and lianas all year round?

It was probably a bit of both—or all three—but for me the important thing is not so much *why* they had this bias, but what *effect* the bias had. In preferring evergreen trees and trying to exclude deciduous trees, Clutterbuck and Griessen and Locke and Sir George Birdwood were all making a simple but fundamental ecological miscalculation.

In a dry climate such as Delhi's where there's no rainfall for up to nine months in the year, the way in which a tree adapts to prolonged drought is to 'shut down' by shedding its leaves. It's a tree's way of coping with prolonged drought. Deciduousness is an entirely *appropriate* adaptive response to Delhi's climate in general, and the sharp seasonality of Delhi's rainfall in particular.

Trees like the imli, arjun, neem or Buddha's coconut behave like broadleaf evergreens when they are growing in moist conditions. When brought to Delhi, however, they are forced to try and cope with a long dry period when little or no rain falls. And they adapt by dropping their leaves in order to stop transpiring moisture during the difficult period when there's no water available.

In India the *same* tree is often found to be deciduous in dry conditions and evergreen in a more moist situation. This seems to be an ecological phenomenon that completely eluded the people who planned avenue trees in the new capital. The jamun and the arjun were chosen because they were considered to be evergreen. And indeed if you travel through a dry forest in central India or in the sub-Himalayan tract, you will find that these trees are indeed evergreen. But look closely at where they are growing—they are classic riparian trees and the only reason they are able to stay green in the dry season is that they grow along river courses where water is always available. Growing along a riverbank, an arjun is not stressed for moisture and it can and will keep its leaves throughout the year.

Bring the arjuns and jamuns to Delhi, however, and they start behaving deciduously, because the climate *forces* them to behave like the rest of Delhi's native trees. So the people who planned New Delhi's avenue trees selected species like the arjun and the jamun which they *believed* to be evergreen. But they did not take into account that these species, which grow in moist conditions, would behave *deciduously* in Delhi's dry climate.

I find it quite extraordinary that a forester like Clutterbuck could make this mistake. He went so far as to make a case for planting the safed siris (*Albizia procera*) in Delhi, which he singled out as the only *Albizia* which was evergreen. But the safed siras grows in swampy ground at the base of the Shivaliks (where it is called the 'doon siras'), and it doesn't take a great deal of experience or insight to see that if you were to take the doon siras out of its swampy context and plant it in Delhi, it will behave just like the other *Albizias*, or perhaps even more deciduously, because it is adapted to having water *all* the year round.

So they got it wrong, in some ways. And we live today with the unintended consequences of a planting scheme that was meant to pan out rather differently. At the same time, if we undertook an audit of the tree species planted in Lutyens' Delhi to try and assess how they have performed—provided you accept that deciduousness is an entirely forgivable shortcoming—many of the trees have actually 'worked' rather well.

This is probably not how Clutterbuck or Lutyens or Griessen or Hardinge might have viewed things if they had been alive today, but based entirely on my subjective judgement, here's a quick report card:

The six mainline species pass with flying colours for their form, appearance and hardiness (even though *all* of them are more or less deciduous). On the debit side, the neem has proved to be surprisingly brittle and vulnerable in violent windstorms, so a few points need to be docked there. And I shudder to think of what will happen to the two riparian species (jamun and arjun) when Delhi's water-table plummets any further. But let's just leave the future out, for the time being, shall we?

The jamun—and to a lesser extent the arjun—is noticeably stunted compared with the way these two trees grow in their natural environment. And especially so in the 'gallery forest' conditions that are mimicked when these trees are planted in avenues. Both trees so clearly indicate their preference for growing in the open, where competition is limited (the jamuns along Rajpath; the arjuns in parks). This is also true of the African sausage tree.

The imlis look their loveliest in new leaf, but they might be in a spot of trouble. We know that Delhi lies towards the very edge of the frost zone and imlis do not tolerate frost well. Global warming could help, but something else is clearly wrong because we have been having unexpectedly high rates of imlis dying on Akbar Road.

The five less common species have done reasonably well, and in retrospect it seems a pity that some of them were not planted more extensively. Three of them are figs, and while the planners might have been understandably nervous about using fig trees (whose roots are near the surface and are notorious for playing havoc with sidewalks), all three of them have done remarkably well in Delhi. The mahua is another outstanding tree that was only planted along one avenue. In new leaf in particular it is one of the most striking avenue trees in New Delhi. But it is impossible not to notice how stunted Delhi's avenue mahuas are.

The third category of rarely planted trees—six species in all—has a spotty report card. The anjan was an inspired choice and in my opinion has proved to be Delhi's most spectacularly beautiful avenue tree. The usba—another fig—has done outstandingly well, too. But there are failures here too—notably, Buddha's coconut, which craves more moisture, and the Ozzy river red gum, which seems sadly cabinned and cramped on a curbside. It is already a relict tree on Tolstoy Marg.

So are there lessons to be learned from which trees have worked well and those that haven't? New Delhi's avenue trees demonstrate eloquently how important it is to plant *with* native ecology, not in defiance of it. But they also remind us how lovely some of the unusual forest trees can be—the anjan and baheda in particular.

We need to experiment with *more* trees that are adapted to deal with ecological conditions found in Delhi. And the obvious place to look is in the forests that surround us—in Haryana, Madhya Pradesh, western Uttar Pradesh and in the drier parts of the terai. At a rough count, there are something like 200 species of forest trees out there, of which only perhaps forty or so have been cultivated.

In the second half of the nineteenth century most provincial governments in India prepared 'Manuals of Arboriculture' that were updated every five years with the wisdom of experience. Trees live so much longer than us that if we don't pass on information to later generations we will tend to repeat the same mistakes again and again. If we can revive this practice of recording our experience with trees and also do some intelligent experimentation with forest trees, we will probably improve upon New Delhi's avenue scheme.

If not, we will probably watch as Lutyens' scheme slowly unravels.

Narayani Gupta

Delhi's History as Reflected in Its Toponymy

One of the areas where history and geography intersect is toponymy. In the 1930s, the geography department of Madras published a fascinating series of articles on place names in Madras Presidency. But after Independence, as geographers and historians became preoccupied with national issues, this interest in the regional and local did not find a place in curriculums or research. Sadly, place names in the area we call Delhi have evoked little interest in its inhabitants, and when names are changed, there is seldom any reaction (the one exception being the protest when Connaught Place was renamed Rajiv and Indira Chowk in 1995). Increasingly there is an urgency to the issue, because landscapes change. As the seven cities of Delhi become the single city of the seventy malls, place names get erased overnight in bouts of celebration and commemoration, and frequently get abbreviated to meaningless initials (is MG Road an abbreviation of 'Mahatma Gandhi' or of 'Mehrauli–Gurgaon'?). One of our achievements in sixty years as an independent country has been to destroy many of Delhi's historic names, as well as its historic landscapes and buildings.

With time, landscapes get sedimented over with new meanings and new maps of movement; but the submerged histories resonate at the sound of place names. There are names of places in Delhi which conjure up vanished landscapes—hills, valleys, streams and a wide river, woods and forests. The Ridge, which protected Delhi's settlements from heat and dust for centuries, has been whittled away to three small fragments, but it was once a distinct range of hills. Muradabad Pahari, in today's Vasant Vihar, Paharganj and Pahari Dhiraj in central Delhi, Raisina Pahari on which the President's house stands, Bhojla Pahari which is the base of the Jama Masjid, and Anand Parbat in West Delhi, are reminders of the hills we have lost. Underhill Road looks like a meandering lane in an English village, but is a reference to the northern Ridge. Fragments of the Ridge are kept intact by the tomb of the mysterious Amir Khan that stands on a platform of rocks overlooking Balban's tomb, and by the hilltop temples of Kalka Mandir and Malay Mandir (which destination boards of buses misspell as *malai*, cream, not as *malay*, hill).

Jaweed Ashraf's delightful book *Historical Ecology of India* describes the Ridge as having been thickly forested until in the fourteenth century much of it was cleared and converted to orchards. The cycle of plantation, clearing, replanting and denudation of the Ridge is a story in itself. From the late medieval centuries the forest area, ideal for *shikar*, was in two swathes, from Palam to Malcha, and in Jahan-numa (its lovely name—Image of the World—was changed to Kamala Nehru Ridge). The fourteenth century *kushk* (hunting lodge, kiosk) of Ferozeshah Tughlaq gives the name to Lutyens' Kushak Road. The forests east of Qila Rai Pithaura must also have had a hunting lodge which gave its name to the Kushak Nallah of the Tughlaq period which we can still see meandering from the western Ridge in a sweep to the south and then northward from Satpula to Nizamuddin.

Even as late as 1883, there is a dramatic description of the undulating land of Delhi, and the waters of streams and *nallahs* tumbling violently into the Yamuna. Delhi's landscape had depressions where water collected to make a *jheel*, where birds gathered and people filled their *gharas*. Najafgarh Jheel was only one of many, another large one was Tal-katora (bowl-shaped tank), yet another was Suraj Kund (sun tank). As the population of the settlements in Delhi grew, and more water was needed, larger tanks were dug out, and channels laid to connect *hauz*/storage-points—at Hauz Shamsi, Hauz Khas, and Hauz Rani (it is possible that Hauz Qazi was older than the Shahjahanabad it is now located in). In the last few decades, the jheels have been indiscriminately filled up with rubble to make land level for construction, and at least two of the hauz are dry land.

Baolis (step-wells) were built to store rainwater and to serve as public places; people gathered on the water-cooled platforms of Sukhi, Gandak and Ugrasen ki Baoli, and innumerable others, since filled up and levelled. Khari Baoli (the well of brackish water) has given its name to a place. Wells also gave their names to places such as Lal Kuan and Dhaula Kuan. It has been suggested that Panchkuian (five wells) was a structure to regulate the flow of water. From the end of the thirteenth century, a network of canals was laid out—the Najafgarh Nahar and the Barapula Nahar were two of these, to which were added, in the seventeenth century, in the city of Shah Jahan, the Ali Mardan Nahar, the Nahar Saadat Khan and, in the palace, the Nahar-e-Bihisht. *Puls* (bridges) have become place-names—the Tughlaq Satpula, the Mughal Athpula and Barapula, named for the number of their arches. When the British built the wall around Shahjahanabad, the name of Badru Gate became Mori (water channel) Gate, because the canal entered the city at that point. On the banks of the Yamuna, *ghats* (flights of shallow steps) were constructed—two being Nigambodh Ghat and Raj Ghat. A point where boats could offload goods was the Tughlaq market of Daryaganj (river market).

Now the nahars are dry nallahs, their unkempt appearance leading to people using them to dump the ubiquitous plastic bags, and the puls are bridges to nowhere. What a landscape could be created by an imaginative team of engineers, planners and designers reviving the canal system and designing green verges and walkways!

In the Delhi region, parts of which were naturally fertile, and where skilful engineering was commissioned to provide water from great distances for irrigation, agriculture was viable, and many small settlements developed, sometimes organically, sometimes by design. Some bore names which were given by the groups of people who came and settled there. In some cases, they carried the name of a village they had left, and gave it to the place they settled in. There are some beautiful names which might well have originated elsewhere, or had a meaning in a local dialect. Many villages have names as unclear of meaning as 'Delhi' itself—Holambi, Mehrauli, Kondli, Mundhela, Okhla, Jasola, Jharoda, Malcha, Munirka, Karkari, Karkardooma, Karari, Dhulsiras, Palam, Hastsal.

More recently, in the early nineteenth century, when Thomas Metcalfe appropriated the land of Chandrawal village to build his stately home, the villagers had to relocate unwillingly to a site further north which they named Chandrawal.

Settlements often got an identity and a name after their land was given as a grant by the ruler. Most of these date from the fifteenth century, when the Lodi kings gave gifts from the *khalsa* (royal) lands in the Delhi area to a large number of nobles. These inami grants were discrete revenue units and can be identified by the suffix '*pur*'—a Sanskrit word indicating a settlement, not necessarily a town, and in some cases even a neighbourhood in a town. The settlements had prefixes usually drawn from a person's name—Badar, Mohammad, Mahipal, Masud, Babar, Humayun, Ali, Begum, Jaisingh. (A locality in New Delhi, Jangpura, is a twentieth-century *pur*—it was named for Mr Young, Delhi's Deputy Commissioner at the time the villagers of Raisina were being resettled in this location.) Some were known from an official's designation, as in Shahpur or Wazirpur. The village named for the Rajput Rai Sina reminds one of the twelfth-century

Rai Pithaura. Nizamuddin Auliya's *khanqah* was in Ghiyaspur, a village named after Ghiyasuddin Tughlaq, the Sultan with whom the saint had come into confrontation. Today there are nearly 100 village enclaves in the National Capital Territory with the suffix '*pur*'. There were many more, which have disappeared in the renaming by the Delhi Development Authority (DDA) and the Municipal Corporation of Delhi (MCD) when they became 'urban extensions'.

The Persian suffix *abad* implied a township—as in Ghaziabad, Faridabad, Muradabad and of course Shahjahanabad. The prefixes were names of individuals, which means that the neighbourhood in east Delhi called Paschimabad is not authentic.

Townships often have second names, sometimes to distinguish land types—*baangar* (hilly/field for grazing), *khaadar* (alluvial land), as in Chilla Saroda Baangar and Chilla Saroda Khaadar, or to distinguish the main village and its younger sibling—*kalan* (large) and *khurd* (small) as in Dariba Kalan and Dariba Khurd (dariba probably indicates an older village name), or a caste divide, as in Saadatpur Musulman and Saadatpur Gujraan.

Villages vary in antiquity, as in social composition. The inhabitants of each village share a clan name—as for example, 'Tokas' for Munirka, 'Panwar' for Shahpur Jat, 'Mehlawat' for Chiragh Delhi—here is a field for social history, as also in listing the groups of the *chaubisi* units of the Jats, which links twenty-four (*chaubees*) villages occupied by a single clan, found in south Delhi villages contiguously located. Unfortunately the blanket term 'urban villages' that the DDA uses for rural settlements incorporated into urban Delhi flattens out many separate and some linked histories. Each village has a separate story: of groups of people settling there; of being deserted because of famine or epidemic; of new irrigation channels and garden-houses and orchards laid out, then deserted, repopulated, then 'regulated' by the Archaeological Survey of India (most of them in the 1920s and 1930s) because there is a 'monument' among its buildings;

of being stripped of its fields by the DDA which privileges urban neighbourhoods over agriculture; of reinventing itself as an adjunct to the same urban neighbourhood by providing services such as domestic helps, smiths, electricians and plumbers; and now moving towards a Disneyland gentrification with boutiques and exotic eateries.

In two interesting senses relations between urban and rural in the Delhi area have not changed in centuries—one, in that villages serviced towns, and two, that they represented different cultures. If the village enclaves today service urban neighbourhoods, in earlier times they provided grain, vegetables, and milk products to the city. Equally, the city inhabitants were insecure because they saw themselves as a separate culture, and as pitted against the rural hinterland. The city was fortified by massive walls not just against possible attack from enemies from afar but against villagers—Meos, Gujjars, Jats—in the vicinity. Therefore, scattered among the *purs* are the *kots*. Today the neighbourhoods install railings and locked gates against the villages.

Kot is Sanskrit for a fort, and the suffix *la* reduces it (like 'city' and 'citadel'). The Tomar Lalkot was built at a height, on the southern Ridge, like all Rajput forts. Kotla Ferozeshah was the fortified citadel at the north end of Ferozeshah Tughlaq's large city, which extended from the river to Mehrauli. The Sayyids who followed the Tughlaqs preferred a more central position for their fort—Kotla Mubarakpur.

The Arabic word *qila* first appears in the context of Prithviraj's fort, Qila Rai Pithaura—and it may well have been the term used not locally but by the army of Muhammad Ghori. Some of the forts that today evoke Mughal grandeur have lost the sense of their original names. Humayun's Dinpanah ('refuge of the faithful') became 'Purana Qila' in the nineteenth century, at the same time as Shah Jahan's Qila Mubarak ('blessed fort') became the more literal Lal Qila. *Garh/garhi*, again Sanskrit for fort, is used as a suffix in Kishengarh / Ballabhgarh / Najafgarh / Himmatgarh / Maidangarhi, and, with a forgotten prefix in Garhi. Mapping forts and seeing their location in relation to the river and water channels would be a fascinating exercise in historical geography.

The gates of the forts were outward-looking, most of them named for the direction they faced—Badayun, Ajmer, Lahore, Kashmir, Dilli (the last a gate in the southern wall of Shahjahanabad, referring to Mehrauli, which the people of Shahjahanabad called 'Dehli'/Dilli).

The term *urdu* refers to the army, hence Urdu Bazaar (perhaps a neighbourhood in Feroze Tughlaq's city which was later incorporated into Shahjahanabad), and Urdu Mandir for the temple built outside Shahjahan's fort for Jain soldiers. Wholesale markets outside city walls may have become neighbourhoods but the names continue—as in Malkaganj, Paharganj and Sabzi Mandi. In some cases ganj may not have indicated a market, but a neighbourhood—as in Trevelyanganj, a neat gridiron suburb laid out by Mr Trevelyan, and Kishenganj, laid out by Diwan Kishan Lal, both in the early nineteenth century. South of Shahjahanabad were Aliganj, part of the fief of Safdarjang, and Raja ka Bazaar, property of the Jaipur raja (later to become part of British New Delhi). Sarais, where travellers and merchants and their pack animals could rest for the night, were located at a distance of seven to eight miles from each other. Around Shahjahanabad were the sarais named Yusuf, Sheikh, Ber, Kale Khan, Badarpur, Julena (named after a European lady who was tutor to the sons of Emperor Aurangzeb), Ruhela, and Badli. In the city, near Chandni Chowk, was the beautifully designed sarai named after its benefactor Princess Jahanara; this name has disappeared because on its site was built, after the Revolt of 1857, the Town Hall.

A curious story is that of the 4000 or more katras (enclosed markets) in Shahjahanabad today, for most part owned by the government. There were very few of these before Partition—Kashmiri Katra and Neel Katra being two of the better-known ones. How did this exponential increase happen? After 1947 many havelis belonging to Muslim families who had migrated to Pakistan were occupied by families of 'refugees' who used them as homes-cum-workshops. In the survey by the Bharat Sevak Samaj prepared shortly after Partition, these were listed as katras, and they continued to be called thus. Like katras, in the city there were not many chowks (an open area at the point of intersection of three or four roads). Saadullah and Chandni Chowk were two major ones—the sense of the first was lost when it disappeared in the clearing of an area around the Fort in 1858, that of the latter when the name began to be used for a whole street (with 'Chandni' becoming 'Chandi'; the malaprop British made Moonlight Square into Silver Street, as can be found in many older guidebooks). 'Indira Chowk' is a malapropism too, because it refers not to an open space but to a circle of buildings facing outward.

If the area south of Shahjahanabad was studded with purs, nineteenth century maps show the west and north as well as the south as laid out with gardens. Very few survive in names today. Those that do are Jorbagh, Sunehri Bagh, Mochi Bagh, Karaul Bagh, Roshanara, Shalimar and Maharani.

Some of the patron deities and saints of Delhi have given their names to localities—the dargahs of Hazrat Nizamuddin to a basti (originally Ghiyaspur village) and of Hazrat Chiragh Dilli to a village, though those of Qutbuddin Bakhtiyar Kaki and Baqibillah have not given their names to localities. The thirteenth century saint Turkman is commemorated as a city gateway. The deity Kalkaji again is the name of a locality, though Jogmaya is not.

Place names and street names are fundamentally different. The first have, for the most part, been given by people who lived there. In the Delhis of the past, places had names, but streets did not. Even when places did not have names, they had easily recognized landmarks. The Pakistani writer Intezaar Husain identified his home in Delhi in a way that he thought made it perfectly easy to locate—it was in a *gali* that had a mango tree. By contrast, streets are usually conferred names by the powers that be, often with an announcement, a plaque and an inauguration. All this began with the English, in whose own country it had begun with Renaissance town planning.

Until 1857 the British contribution to names in Delhi was minimal. Stately British homes, like Indian havelis, was distinguished by the owners' names—Ludlow Castle and Metcalfe House being well-known examples. Some Indianized sahibs liked poetic names, and when Metcalfe turned Quli Khan's tomb in Mehrauli into a country-house he called it Dilkusha (heart's delight), and Ochterlony named his garden in north Delhi Mubarak Bagh (blessed garden). The British military station on the northern Ridge by contrast had functional names on signposts like Racquet Court Road and Cavalry Lines. Memories of battles in distant places led to the break in the northern Ridge being called Khyber Pass.

From 1858, the city was reshaped into a cantonment and a municipality; many streets were cut through Shahjahanabad, and street-lamps and paving were introduced; the area north of the city was laid out into a spacious civil station. This was the beginning of a long saga of building extensive roads in Delhi. Commemoration and street naming went together. In marked contrast to the older destination names, Alipur, Rajpur, Qutb, Mathura, were the new Nicholson Road, Queens Road, Lothian Road, and Elgin Road. While Nicholson was given a road in Shahjahanabad, other military heroes of 1857 were commemorated in the cantonment, making it a clone of cantonments all over India. The sense of a spacious sub-city led to the Civil Lines being bordered by The Mall (Indianised into 'Mall Road'). Kingsway Camp was given its name at the time of the 1911 Durbar.

From 1914 to 1931, the first wholly British Indian city was designed and laid out. The city designed by Edwin Lutyens was a vast network of streets and avenues with a few small buildings scattered along them. By contrast to the richly-textured Shahjahanabad (or for that matter old towns like Paris or London), where public thoroughfares were animated because of a dense web of activities, British New Delhi—till the 1960s—was a desert of wide empty streets.

When it came to naming them, there was a depressing lack of imagination. The nationalist agitation of the 1920s prompted a need to remind visitors of the imperial nature of British rule while at the same time showing it as the last in a series of powerful rulers. New Delhi was seen as part of a succession of dynastic capitals (hence Windsor Place, though no one thought to name the 'eighth' Delhi, successor to Shahjahanabad, 'Georgetown'). The numbingly boring Kingsway and Queensway were repeated in King George's Avenue and Queen Mary's Avenue. The names could have reflected New Delhi, built in a mixture of Indian and Western styles of architecture, as part of a long cultural tradition now tempered with an infusion from the West. The opportunity was lost. It was not Aristotle, Kalidas and Shakespeare whom roads were named after, but Prithviraj, Asoka, Ferozeshah Tughlaq, Akbar and Aurangzeb. Dynasties shared space in Lodi Road and Tughlaq Road, though every Viceroy got a look in and, in a fit of generosity, so did the French Dupleix and the Portuguese Albuquerque. The Raja of Jaipur had contributed the land for the capital (Jaisinghpura and Raisina), therefore Rajas Man Singh and Jai Singh got a road apiece. In a magnanimous gesture, officials and engineers—Hailey, Rouse and Keeling were allotted wide roads while Lutyens got what was no better than a lane. No sooner had all this been settled than along came Vicereine Lady Willingdon who named everything she laid eyes on after her family—the Viceroy's name for Airport, Stadium, Hospital and Crescent, her own for a Park (after Independence, it was renamed Lodi Garden), and her relatives remembered in Brassey Road and Ratendon Road.

In 1947–49, as the dislocated people from Pakistan poured into Delhi, the map of the district was opened out and the surrounding *nuzul* villages (owned by the municipality) circled as the cheapest option for sites for rehabilitation. The village names disappeared and a series of 'nagars' named for heroes of the nationalist movement were laid out—Malviya, Lajpat, Jawahar, Kamala, Subhash, Rajendra, Patel . . . The name of Chittaranjan Das was later given to what was known for an unnecessarily long period as EPDP ('East Pakistan Displaced Persons') Colony, while immigrants from the North West Frontier Province were settled in neighbourhoods named for towns of that province—Dera Ismael Khan and Gujranwala. Roads also celebrated the heroes of 1857—the Rani of Jhansi and Bahadur Shah 'Zafar'. Todarmal and Abul Fazl (ministers of Akbar's court) were given *jagirs,* though not near Akbar Road. Original Road became Deshbandhu Gupta Road, Old Mill Road was renamed after Rafi Ahmad Kidwai as Rafi Marg.

As the statues of viceroys and British military heroes were removed from parks and public squares, and relocated or sold, the roads named for viceroys and generals began to be painted over. Little Kasturba Gandhi to her surprise found herself stepping into Curzon's seven-league boots, and for some unknown reason Copernicus was pulled back from the contemplation of the planets to replace Lytton. King George's Avenue, in a pun noticed by Laura Sykes, became Raja-ji Road. The formidable General Roberts stepped down for three unknown soldiers— the Teen Murti. The terrible Nicholson survived by oversight twice over—as a road in the city as well as in the cantonment. With a doubtful sense of justice, Dupleix was allowed to stay but Albuquerque has been defeated, his road now named 'Tees (30) January Marg' to mark the date in 1948 when Mahatma Gandhi was assassinated in a house on that road. Over the years, as the powers that be (I am told that the Road Names Committee is chaired by the Chief Minister) pulled out and checked their school history books, further refinements were made. Sanskritification entered, with the use of *marg* and *veethi*; in the same narrow spirit, *sadak* was not used.

People in Delhi tend to categorize individuals by localities. Jug Suraiya in his delightful article about the Delhi Question, 'Where are you putting up?' saw this as a symptom of snobbery. But we have learned to circumvent this by making it difficult to place people. As in so much else, we have now learned the art of 'duplicating' place names. Next time someone says they live in Panchsheel Park, if you are snobbish about such things, you would be wise to ask whether it is near Shahdara or near Siri Fort. Of course the Siri Fort Panchshila Park inhabitants had obfuscated things even earlier by pronouncing the word as Panchsheel (the first is Five Stones, the second Five Principles) in order to be deliberately confused with Panchsheel in Chanakyapuri, the Diplomatic Enclave, an address which we would all love to flaunt. One embarrassing measure was the choice of attributes to differentiate housing-complexes of officials of different levels in the hierarchy— Man, Shan, Vinay and Seva (greatness, grandeur, humility and service). The occupants of Vinay Nagar saw red, protested vociferously and had their colony's name changed, and this so unnerved their 'superior' officers that they decided to shed their *maan* and *shaan* and become Rabindra (Rabindranath Tagore) and Bharati (Subramania Bharathi). The renaming of Seva Nagar as Kasturba Nagar, significantly, has not been reflected in popular perception, and sadly the 'colony' continues to be called Seva.

Delhi grew exponentially from the 1960s—by expansion and by infill. Names like South End, West End, North End and East End indicate a sense of limits, as Western Extension Area and South Extension suggest extensions beyond those limits. Choices for road names went beyond the national and historic to the international and contemporary, and even to the level of ideals. The diplomatic triumph of the Panchsheel Pact of 1954 led to the five Buddhist principles becoming road names—Niti, Nyaya, Shanti, Satya and Dharma—optimistically located in the spacious Diplomatic Enclave which was named Chanakyapuri. As if to emphasize the point they also, for good measure, threw in a Kautilya Marg (Kautilya and Chanakya being the same person, India's fourth century BC philosopher of statecraft). The Non-Aligned Movement gave us Josip Broz Tito Marg and Gamal Abdul

Nasser Marg, while a general spirit of international goodwill brought Simon Bolivar, Benito Juarez, Olof Palme, Che Guevara, Nelson Mandela and Archbishop Makarios. Incidentally, one wonders what has become of Ho Chi Minh, until recently controlling a section of the Outer Ring Road? Roads in Defence Colony (where the houses belonged to retired armed forces personnel) recalled the war-horses of mythology—Bhishma Pitamah and Drona.

Later, meticulous idealism became less pronounced, and a certain degree of carelessness could be seen in the naming of places. Africa Avenue, alliteratively pleasing but aligning absurdly unequal scales, is just one example of this. There are streets with utilitarian names which could legitimately be given evocative new names—Mandir Marg, Church Road, Teen Murti Marg. (The last was the location of our first Prime Minister's house, while the present one has a sporty address totally at variance with his personality—Race Course Road.)

Road and place names are arbitrarily chosen and changed, never explained. (Who was Bhagwandas, why Sikandra Road, who is the Srinivas of Srinivaspuri, whose uncle was remembered in Kaka Nagar, whose father in Bapa Nagar?) (There is the other fascinating avenue to explore—the increasing popularity of names like Oxford, Piccadilly and Manhattan—but that is a story in itself, briefly and delightfully addressed by the French anthropologist Dr Veronique Dupont.) Neither officials nor citizens use the names of roads. Directions are usually based on some 'main road' and a PVR or mall. A friend in Gulmohur Park once gave me clear directions—'Drive past Amitabh Bachchan's house, then turn left at the garbage dump'. Obviously, we can't afford to clean up Delhi—we'll lose all sense of direction.

As green cover and water bodies give way to tarmac and concrete, the sense of rivers and parks is invoked in names. In the neighbourhood called Alakananda, where the waters and hills of India meet, geography has run wild: Gangotri, Yamuna, Mandakini, Kaveri and Nilgiri. An undulating range of low hills with high aspirations was named Kailash. It spawned Greater Kailash which multiplied into Part 1, 2, 3 and 4, Kailash Hills and Greater Kailash Enclaves, swallowing up a corner of Masjid Moth Revenue Estate. This Estate (which stretched from South Extension to Chittaranjan Park), was auctioned in lots, and over time sections of it reinvented themselves as a series of green spaces—Uday Park, Neeti Bagh, Gulmohur Park and Panchsheel Park. Today 'Masjid Moth' remains the name for the Estate's two extremities, that next to South Extension and that near Chittaranjan Park. Piety leads to neighbourhoods being named after sacred cities, as in Dwarka and Saket.

What is missing is the individuals whom we should remember. In Kolkata, one emerges from Netaji Subhash Chandra Bose Airport on to Kazi Nazrul Islam Sarani, and one can almost hear echoes of Nazrul-geethi. In Delhi, Indira Gandhi Airport opens on to NH8. Suppose it was called Amir Khusro Sadak—what an echo it would find in people from so many countries! But, in keeping with the British sense of Delhi as a political city with a political history, artists and writers are not the names that first come to mind when a road or neighbourhood has to be named. The only artist who has been honoured is Amrita Sher Gil, the only literary figure Rabindranath Tagore. The great literary figure K.K. Nair, whose pen-name was Krishna Chaitanya, lived on the road which later was given that name—but not, as one would have thought, to honour him; this refers to Chaitanya Mahaprabhu, a medieval saint. There are the noble exceptions—the initiative of St. Stephen's College led to a teacher's name being immortalized as Sudhir Bose Road, while Safdar Hashmi Marg reminds us of a great human being and a talented artist whose life was cruelly cut short.

Many books have been written on Delhi, many of them going over the same ground but without turning up the earth. Historians look back at Delhi as a series of cities planned by whimsical rulers, planners look forward to a Delhi where the dying Ridge will be compensated by flyovers and elevated rail-lines, where the riverbed will be treated as real estate, where all neighbourhoods will look alike and hubs of interaction will be segregated from places where people live. This will be the death of the Indian city of Delhi as we know it. Historians and planners have a duty to stop it from dying. Students of history can each fill in a little piece of the jigsaw puzzle that Delhi is, by exploring its localities, its multiple histories, the story of many migrations, of times of feasts and times of famine, of city-building and of planting gardens and sowing crops. Planners could learn much wisdom from the past, and ensure a seamless continuity to this historic city, instead of calculated breaks. Let us admit that for us all, *Dilli dur ast*. Let us try to get nearer to it.

Notes

I wish to thank Niharika Gupta for her encouragement, and for helping remove infelicities in my prose.

Narayani Gupta

Vidya Rao

The Dilli Gharana

Gharanas are families of musicians whose members are linked by ties of blood but, even in the past and increasingly now, the gharana also includes disciples unrelated by blood to the core gharana family. As the word suggests, musical gharanas are families—'real' or fictive. The ties between ustad and shagird (disciple), even in the absence of an actual blood tie, are as those of parent and child.

How do gharanas come into being? Joan Erdman suggests that a gharana comes into being as a result of 'desi' voices singing margi music. Here, the marg, or the formal notion of what music is, gets inflected in quite specific ways by the voices of the people of the region imparting it a localized flavour. Other factors contribute to the importance of certain ragas and compositions—these then become typical of the musical style and repertoire of the gharana. Implicit in this view is the understanding of music itself and how it is to be categorized. Indian music (or any other art form) resists categorization into clear categories such as folk/classical/popular etc. These categories arise from and are perhaps more applicable to western thought (though even in the west these are now questioned).

Indian musical systems display considerable overlap of contexts, personnel and styles; thus clear cut (and one might say, somewhat dualistic) categories do not so easily apply here. Thus Ashok Ranade prefers to classify Indian musical forms differently—as community music, art music etc. Gharana music could be seen as one of the forms of art music, where a professional community of persons welds itself into a kind of guild, develops styles and techniques specific to itself (often guarding these from outsider-others), and transmits this knowledge formally from one generation to the next. Such transmission is often accompanied by rituals and a certain formality, and not everyone can become an accepted disciple of the gharana. The gharana's wisdom (for indeed singers refer to the repertoire and its techniques and world-view as 'ilm'—knowledge/wisdom) is equally its (somewhat intangible, but very real for all that) wealth.

Bandish compositions are often referred to as *cheez* (quite literally, 'things') and are handed down by ustads, and received with the utmost respect by disciples. Both ustads and shagirds are aware of the enormity of this gift of knowledge. In addition, the sharing of the corpus of bandishes (musical compositions) and the singing style creates a sense of identity, a feeling of community; this is so even when there is no actual blood or other tie. This is a sense of 'family' then that transcends that of kinship in the usual sense of the term; it is a family based on ties of knowledge and the shared inheritance of that knowledge.

Ethnomusicologists like Daniel Neuman hold that the growth of gharanas is linked to the rise of urban centres—centres of sustained patronage for the arts. The understanding here is that wherever there have been urban centres, wherever there have been courts, there one has indeed found patrons of the arts, and a situation where the arts have been able to flourish for generations. Such a situation encourages the rise and growth of a gharana—a musical lineage.

Gharana refers primarily to a vocal style but often the gharana may also include various instruments. The Dilli gharana, for instance, is also noted for its sarangi playing, and one of the greatest masters of the sarangi, Ustad Bundu

Khan, belonged to this gharana. There is also a tabla baaj (or style of playing tabla) which is associated with the Dilli gharana.

There are several gharana traditions that exist today, each displaying a specific style of singing and of voice production. Each has its own marked characteristics, and growing out of these, its repertoire of preferred ragas and bandish-compositions that reflect the genius of the gharana's style. Among these is the Dilli gharana. Delhi has been, for centuries, a hub of political power and artistic patronage. Its glittering courts have been adorned by many great artists. Quite naturally, Delhi has been home to a rich gharana tradition. While many consider Gwalior to be the oldest gharana, there are others who hold that Dilli's tradition is even older than Gwalior's.

Returning to Erdman's position—that gharanas arise out of desi voices singing margi music. What we are being alerted to here, is that a musical style grows out of the soil in which it finds itself. There is an accepted notion of what music is. This includes basic ideas of the organization of musical sound into ragas (even when, as in community songs, this understanding may be very rudimentary, the incipient raga structures may remain unnamed, the raga may not appear in its 'pure' form, and it may not be treated to a detailed elaboration). But the basic understanding remains the same. There is a basic shared understanding, too, of how musical time is to be organized into tala patterns that are cyclical rather than linear. Here again, in different forms, these tala patterns are performed differently, different instruments might be used etc. This overarching path of musical understanding might be called the marg. It needs however to be brought to life—embodied, as it were—by the singing voice.

Desi refers to the notion of the region, the specific space (and moment) where marg music may be actually sounded and heard. The word desi is often used as a sort of substitute for the word 'folk music'. Understanding desi as the regional or the specific, however, invites us to look at this a little differently. Desi music is the music of the region. It is the music as sung by the people of that region with their specific throw of voice (surely itself influenced by the local landscape), their specific languages and oriented to their specific personal and social needs.

Forms are now not so easily categorized into 'folk' or 'classical'. Nor can they be arranged in a hierarchy. What we have instead is a lateral spread, one where the defining boundaries between forms become porous, and forms themselves acquire a certain fluidity. We might also now categorize forms in terms of contexts of performance (where is this being sung?), personnel involved (who sings and who listens?), and indeed, even, the intention of the performance (why is this performance taking place?). What is being sung, and how, will be influenced greatly by the above three factors. This is what Erdman implies when she speaks of the desi voices singing marg sangeet. A gharana's musicians draw from the generally accepted notion of what music is, what voice is. But the specific singing style is deeply influenced by regional sounds, speech patterns and intonation, existing poetic traditions of the region etc.

A gharana's musical identity seems also to be created by the coming together of different forms performed in different contexts and for different reasons. Devotional music (whether of the institutionalized type such as the music of the temples, or the music of wandering mystics) is one such source. Another are the songs of the community/communities of the region—the regional 'folk' tradition—songs of the household, songs that mark moments in the life cycle, work songs, songs that mark the seasons and annual events. Along with these, there also exists an overarching understanding of what music is, the notion of raga and tala and the philosophical underpinnings of raga sangeet. When these come together a specific style is created—a style typical of the region. It is therefore not without reason that gharanas are generally known by the name of the region in which they grow and flourish, for indeed it is the region, and the sounds of that region—the desi soundscape—that give a gharana its specific character.

In thinking of gharanas thus we are alerted to another fact—that patronage of the arts is of many kinds, and it takes place through many agencies and in many spaces. The music of life cycle rituals sung by women in the household has, apparently, no official patronage. Yet it is nurtured by the community and kept alive. The songs are part of the community's inheritance, identity and sense of belonging. In a sense, each person who joins in the singing of a sohar (birth song) or a kajri (songs sung in the rains and often also offered to the goddess Vindhyavasini Devi) is by the very act of singing, ensuring a kind of unspoken, unlauded patronage for the music. So too the music offered at temples and dargahs (sufi shrines) is sung in the spirit of sewa or hazri dena; it is an offering made to the deity/saint. In the dargahs, the mehfil-e-sama takes place every Thursday. In the temples of the Pushtimarga tradition of Krishna worship, raga sewa (the offering of music) is an integral part of the temple rituals which comprise three main aspects—raga, bhog, and shringar (offering the deity music, feeding him, and adorning his form). These ritualized sewas are performed no less than eight times in a day (nitya-sewa), while special sewas are performed at festivals (varsh-sewa). Music is an integral part of every sewa and it is a highly structured repertoire that is sung by special temple kirtankars. In this way, this music too was, over the centuries, kept alive, patronized—though this was not courtly patronage.

Speaking of the Dilli gharana, of which he is the current Khalifa, Ustad Iqbal Ahmed Khan points out that the Dilli gharana displays two simultaneous streams of musical focus: the sufiana, and the darbari—the music inspired by the sufic traditions, and that inspired by the courtly temperament. Iqbal Khan Saheb's description thus includes both courtly and institutionalized religious musical styles and the formalized patronage of these. In his singing, and in his descriptions of the many song-styles included in his gharana's repertoire, we also see that this repertoire includes forms that draw from folk traditions of the region.

Ustad Iqbal Ahmed Khan traces the beginnings of the Dilli gharana to the thirteenth century to the court of Shamsuddin Altamash (Iltumish) who ruled from 1211 to 1236. Altamash's court was home to two singers—Mir Hasan Sawant and Mir Bula Kalawant.

Mir Hasan Sawant was of a spiritual temperament. Great singer though he was, he left the court and became a disciple, a murid of Khwaja Muinuddin Chishti (who lived from 1138/39 to 1236). Khwaja Muinuddin Chishti had himself adapted the local traditional musical style of kirtan singing, infusing it with sufi philosophy and the sounds and vocal flavours of central and west Asia, to create a new form, qawwali. Miya Sawant, as Khwaja Muinuddin's disciple, learnt this new style and sang these compositions. Thus he became the first sufi classical singer.

Mir Bula Kalawant, on the other hand, remained at the court as a rajgavaiya (court musician) and continued to sing the older, traditional gayaki of dhrupad-dhamar.

Mir Hasan Sawant was followed by his son and grandson, Miya Shams Sawant and Miya Saamti Qawwal. The latter was a murid (disciple) of Hazrat Nizamuddin Auliya (1238–1325), and was thus a guru bhai—a brother, by virtue of sharing a common preceptor—of Hazrat Amir Khusrau. We of course know Amir Khusrau as the beloved disciple of Hazrat Nizamuddin Auliya, and also as a great poet and musician. Amir Khusrau's compositions form a large part of the repertoire of present-day qawwali singing. He is moreover credited with the creation of forms ranging from qawwali to khayal and also for the invention of the tabla and the sitar. He composed his poetry in both Braj Bhasha and Persian and also in a mixed language style where different languages were combined in a single poem. His poems continue to be sung today by singers from different gharanas and in different forms—qawwali, khayal and even thumri.

Not surprisingly, Miya Saamti used to sing all the

compositions of Amir Khusrau. As a result, these compositions became a part of the repertoire of Miya Saamti and after him, of his descendants. The style of singing of Miya Saamti and his lineage was deeply influenced by the gayaki of qawwali. As a result, Miya Saamti's descendants came to be regarded as belonging to the tradition of the Qawwal Bacche. This style of singing flourished down the generations until the time of Miya Achpal, in whose time, the styles and traditions of the Qawwal Bacche and those of the darbari singers (descendants of Mir Bula Kalawant) were fused into one rich gayaki known to us today as the Dilli gharana.

Simultaneously, the qawwali tradition of singing continued in the hands of the Qawwal Bacche.

The fusing of these two streams—the sufiana and the darbari—is seen also in the singing of an early twentieth century singer, Ustad Mamman Khan. He was heir to both these traditions which he inherited through his father's and mother's lineages. Ustad Mamman Khan was descended on his maternal side from the singers of the Qawwal Bacche tradition. His paternal ancestors included Miya Achpal, Miya Achpal's shagird, Tanras Khan, and the brothers Mir Ila Khan and Mir Umrao Khan (sons of Tanras Khan), singers of dhrupad–dhamar. Thus, the sufiana and the darbari came together again in his voice to further refine the composite gayaki that we now speak of as the Dilli gharana.

Because it brought together these two different musical identities, the gayaki of the Dilli gharana exhibits traits quite different from any other gayaki. The gayaki is an extraordinary mix of dhrupad-dhamar, khayal, tarana; it also draws from folk music derived forms such as jhoola geet, sawan geet, banra geet, sehra, suhag geet (music that celebrates the seasons of the earth and of human life), as well as from forms such as qaul, qalbana, dhamaal which claim a sufi ancestry. It also includes forms noted for their technical virtuosity—raga sagar (a composite of seven ragas), tala sagar (a composite of seven talas) etc. Several of the forms sung in the Dilli tradition are practically unknown today—naqsh-o-gul, hawa, basit, savela—and are an interesting example of forms that seem to incorporate qualities of other forms and styles. Thus savela, as sung by Dilli gharana artistes, exhibits voice modulations and modes of elaboration that are almost like thumri.

The darbari or courtly tradition of music of Mir Bula Kalawant received patronage over the centuries despite Delhi's turbulent history. Archival sources mention musicians at the courts of Akbar, Jahangir and Shahjahan, and though Aurangzeb has the dubious distinction of banning music altogether, contemporary musicians do recall bandishes that mention this emperor and praise him. However, at this stage we cannot still speak of a gharana. This is perhaps because the rise of gharanas tends to coincide with the growth of khayal as a form, and moreover as a form that received court patronage. It seems probable that during this time khayal was not yet a courtly form, even if it did exist. Therefore, the questions we might ask here are when did khayal come into existence, and when did it begin to receive court patronage.

There are no clear answers to these questions. Different scholars have different views. Some consider Amir Khusrau (1253–1325) to have developed the form as early as the thirteenth century. Other scholars point to not Delhi at all but Jaunpur and the court of the Sharqi sultans. Yet others draw our attention to the mention of a form called khelapad, mentioned in the thirteenth century musical treatise, *Sangeet Ratnakara*, and claim this to be the first khayal.

The city of Delhi is linked to the development of khayal through the legend of the two brothers Niamat Khan and Feroz Khan, better known by their pen-names of Sadarang and Adarang. Singers at the court of Mohammad Shah Rangile (1719–1748), the compositions of these two musicians still form the mainstay of the repertoire of almost every existing gharana of khayal gayaki. Legend has it that the two brothers incurred the displeasure of the Emperor and fled (or were exiled) to Lucknow where, in secret, they developed a new style of singing. They presented this incognito at Delhi and found favour once more with the Emperor. This new form, khayal, finally came to be accepted as a worthy form to be presented at court.

In the works of Sadarang and Adarang we see again the coming together of two somewhat different styles of poetry, themes and even use of language. Whereas Sadarang's compositions cover a wide variety of themes, including the romantic, and several of his compositions also intertwine his own nom-de-plume with that of his patron-sultan, Adarang's compositions tend to be more philosophical. Again all these aspects—the romantic, the courtly, the pastoral, the deeply philosophical, and even the didactic—are the subjects of khayal's bandishes. Delhi thus has had an important role, if not the central role, to play in the development of khayal gayaki.

There are other stories that are told and that seem to bolster the notion of Dilli gharana as being one of the first gharanas. One such story is about the seventeenth century singers, Haddu Khan and Hassu Khan. Haddu and Hassu Khan are said to be the founders of the Gwalior gharana, which is generally today considered to be the 'mother' gharana. The story goes that these two singers learnt khayal gayaki by eavesdropping on the riyaaz of the singers of the Qawwal Bacche school. Like all legends and stories, this one is interesting, not because it is or is not provable historical fact, but because it suggests ways in which a gharana builds/remembers its past and thus creates its identity, history and, indeed, its sense of legitimacy.

Hearing stories about the old singers, one realizes that the Dilli gharana has influenced several singers from other schools. Ustad Zahoor Khan of the Khurja gharana is one such, who received taleem from Ustad Tanras Khan of the Dilli gharana. Ustad Zahoor Khan was also a great composer of bandishes and compositions in both Brajbhasha and Urdu. His Brajbhasha compositions are signed 'Ramdas' while his Urdu compositions use the taqqalus or pen-name 'Mumkin'. Yet another interesting fact is that the great composer Ustad Mehboob Khan 'Daras Piya' was also a disciple of Ustad

Tanras Khan of the Dilli gharana. And since 'Daras Piya' was the father-in-law of Ustad Fayyaz Khan 'Aftab-e-Mausiqi', doyen of the Agra gharana, there would surely have been some give and take between the Dilli and the Agra gharanas. Further, the founders of the Patiala gharana, Ustad Ali Bux Jarnail and Ustad Fateh Ali, disciples of Mian Kaalu, also sought taleem from, among other ustads, none other than Tanras Khan. Similarly, in the twentieth century, Ustad Bade Ghulam Ali Khan also received taleem from Ustad Ashiq Ali of the Dilli gharana. In practice, therefore, the gharana was not a watertight, sealed-off entity and movements and exchange between gharanas was not only possible, but even considered desirable.

While musicians learnt from each other and from ustads of gharanas other than their own, matrimonial alliances also led to musical exchanges. Thus Ustad Iqbal Ahmed Khan points to his own repertoire, which draws from that of both his maternal and paternal grandfathers. From the maternal side Ustad Iqbal Khan inherited the repertoire and style of Ustad Chand Khan (and through Chand Khan to the repertoire of the latter's father, Ustad Mamman Khan and uncle Ustad Samman Khan). On the paternal side, he drew from the repertoires of Ustad Jahan Khan, Ustad Osman Khan and Ustad Nasir Ahmed Khan.

Another interesting fact is that Bahadur Shah Zafar was himself a shagird of Miya Achpal and therefore, the Emperor of India and Tanras Khan were guru bhais. In the season of Basant, Zafar would travel to Jahaz Mahal in Mehrauli with his retinue. Among them would be Tanras Khan and Miya Achpal. Tanras Khan was then known as Qutab Baksh. He would hold the reins of Miya Achpal's horse, and walk alongside his Ustad. Legend has it that it was on those journeys that, as they travelled, Miya Achpal would give his shagird taleem in a particular tarana. Perfecting this tarana, Qutab Baksh became known as Tanras Khan.

If Rangile's court might be considered the site for the development of khayal gayaki, Zafar's court patronized, among other forms, the poetry and music of the ghazal, both Urdu and Persian. As a result, the Dilli gharana is perhaps the only gharana that includes the ghazal in its repertoire. Even today, several of the leading ghazal singers of the subcontinent claim allegiance to this gharana—among them, Mallika Pukhraj, Farida Khanum and Iqbal Bano. Iqbal Bano was, in fact, a shagird of Ustad Chand Khan.

But Bahadur Shah Zafar was not merely a poet of ghazal. There are also a number of khayal compositions to his credit, including the well-known one in Khamaj-Bahar—*Sakal ban gagan*—a composition that found its way into a popular film. The composer of film music, Roshan, as a shagird of the gharana had learnt this bandish and subsequently used it in a film. Yet another shagird of this gharana from the world of films is the composer Naushad Ali.

As mentioned earlier, folk forms also found their way into the Dilli gharana, as did forms like savela (also called sohla/shohla) that sound almost thumri-like in their manner of voice production and in the particular way of developing the bandish. Savela's poetry and even its gayaki draws from the sufi repertoire of Amir Khusrau. It differs from khayal also in that the bandish generally has more than one antara (the second part of the composition). The Dilli gharana also includes a style called hawa. Musically, this style reflects certain tendencies that were also prevalent at the time in poetry. Hawa is unique in that it brings together different languages/dialects within the same poetic text. Perhaps one of the earliest examples of this is seen in some of the poetry of Amir Khusrau (pointing again to the deep influence of the sufi traditions and styles in the gharana's repertoire). This kind of verse was known in the literary canon as rekhta. One could say that the poetry of hawa/rekhta influenced the growth of the language we now speak—a mix of many dialects and languages. If forms like savela show clear links with the sufi repertoire, a form like tala sagar with its virtuoso flourishes points to the atmosphere of the glittering courts of the nineteenth century. In this complex form, the bandish is set in a garland of talas; it moves from one to the other, finally arriving back at the sam in an astoundingly brilliant climax. The bandish is difficult enough to sing; even more daunting is the prospect of elaborating it and singing improvisatory passages!

Part of the lore surrounding Hazrat Amir Khusrau, and also the Dilli gharana, is that Khusrau is credited with the introduction into Indian music of the raga Bahar. Ustad Iqbal Ahmed Khan explains it thus: The very word 'bahar' is of Persian origin. Hazrat Amir Khusrau introduced this raga and this word into the existing musical repertoire. Not surpisingly, the Dilli gharana has a large number of ragas derived from the basic Bahar—Bahar ke prakar.

Sufi stories also tell us about the singing of raga Bahar by Amir Khusrau. In order to gladden his Pir, Amir Khusrau brought bunches of mustard flowers to him and presented them to him, singing this raga. The famous composition in this raga, *Sakal ban phool rahi sarson*, is thus sung by both the qawwals as well as the khayal singers of the Dilli gharana.

Apart from the vast range of styles of music and poetry, the Dilli gharana is also credited with the invention of several instruments: among them Ustad Mamman Khan's sursagar and Ustad Bundu Khan's small sarangi (called tota).

The gharana includes several illustrious names—Ustad Bundu Khan was Ustad Mamman Khan's nephew and son-in-law and a renowned sarangi nawaaz. Ustad Mamman Khan's elder brother, Ustad Samman Khan was a familiar figure at Jama Masjid. He would go there every day, sit on the steps of the masjid all day—'from asar ka namaz until maghrib ka namaz'—and teach whoever wished to learn. Among those who took taleem from him was Kundan Lal Saigal. Ustad Chand Khan, who adopted Ustad Iqbal Ahmed Khan and brought him up, was the earlier Khalifa of the gharana; after his passing in 1981, Ustad Iqbal Ahmed Khan was declared the Khalifa.

Ustad Nasir Ahmed Khan is yet another artiste of this gharana, as are Ustad Osman Khan, Ustad Hilal Khan, Ustad

Zahoor Khan and Ustad Zafar Ahmed Khan. Contemporary artistes include the sitar maestro Sayeed Zafar, the tabla wizards Shafaat Ahmed Khan (who, sadly, passed away a few years ago at a young age) and Subhash Nirwan, the vocalist Anis Ahmed Khan and the vocalist and musicologist, Dr Krishna Bisht.

While the Khalifa of the khayal tradition of the Dilli gharana is Ustad Iqbal Ahmed Khan, the qawwal tradition too continues to flourish, the Khalifa of that tradition being Ustad Meraj Nizami. The links between the two branches of Delhi's musical tradition are strong, and the Dilli gharana's exponents regularly offer hazri at the shrine of the sufi saints Hazrat Nizamuddin Auliya, Hazrat Amir Khusrau and Hazrat Enayat Khan. And like the khayal tradition, the Qawwal Bacche gayaki also spread to other parts of India. The qawwali singers, the Warsi brothers of Hyderabad, for instance, also claim descent from Ustad Tanras Khan.

Many spaces in Delhi have a long association with the gharana, an example being the Parade Grounds that Bahadur Shah Zafar gifted to Tanras Khan. At that time, this area was known as Khanum ka Bazaar. Bahadur Shah Zafar also gifted Chandni Mahal to Tanras Khan. Members of the gharana continue to live here to this day. The family's connection with Delhi is evident from the fact that the house named Mausiqi Manzil, where Ustad Iqbal Ahmed Khan lives, has been the family's home for 200 years.

Though the gharana's home is in Delhi, and it is known by the name of this city, yet music has no boundaries. The Dilli gharana has even travelled across the border to Pakistan where it continues to be known as the Dilli gharana, despite its different location. Here too, one sees the two streams of khayal and qawwali. One of the finest khayal singers of the subcontinent, Ustad Nasiruddin Sami of Pakistan, claims descent from the Dilli gharana, as does the charismatic qawwali singer Ustad Farid Ayyaz. As we have seen, the ghazal singers Mallika Pukhraj, Farida Khanum and Iqbal Bano—all from Pakistan—are disciples of this gharana. Other

Pakistani artistes like Ustad Sardar Khan, Ustad Chhote Ghulam Ali Khan and Ustad Bahauddin Khan trace their musical lineage through Ustad Tanras Khan to the Qawwal Bacche tradition.

But Ustad Iqbal Ahmed Khan stresses that though the music of the gharana may be heard in other places today, the members of the Dilli gharana were and are children of India. The gayaki of the gharana reflects the syncretic nature of Indian cultural forms, while Chand Khan's reply to Bukhari, then Controller at All India Radio, reflects the gharana's deep roots in Delhi's soil. When asked by Bukhari why he had not migrated to Pakistan, Chand Khan replied through a couplet:

Ke Jamuna nahi hai ja mein, masjid vahan nahi
Sunte ho miya! Hame vahan jana nahi.

There can be no masjid in that land where the Jamuna does not flow
Do you hear me, Sir! I don't want to go there!

Sohail Hashmi

The Language of Delhi: Birth, Growth, Banishment, Reinvention

The following doha from a text on grammar by Hem Chandra illustrates how words from different languages—Punjabi, Saraiki, Gujarati, Rajasthani, Khadi Boli and Braj—were being used simultaneously in poetic works around the tenth century AD:

Bhalaa hua jo maarya, bahini mharaa kanto
Laaj janej toveen si aaho jai bhaga ghar wanto[1]

Dear sister, it is as well that our Kaant died in battle
He would have shamed me no end, had he run away and come home

This is just one of the vast numbers of textual references the awareness or ignorance of whose existence has informed the debate on what was the language that was spoken in Delhi. The theories put across broadly fall into three categories: the first is that there was a time in the indeterminable past when Delhi used to have a language that belonged uniquely to it and that over time that language has ceased to exist primarily due to outside influences; the other opinion insists that Delhi never had a language that could be identified uniquely with it; and the third argues that only a mishmash Creole or pidgin was and continues to be the medium of communication in Delhi.

I think that none of these theories are entirely correct and yet all of them are not entirely wrong. I will try to explain my understanding of the evolution of the language that was spoken in the environs of Delhi and came to be known at different periods as Dehlavi, Zaban-e-Dehli, Hindavi, Rekhta, Hindi and Urdu. Before launching into this narration I wish, however, to make a few general observations about language per se.

Languages survive and grow as long as they are able to change with the changing needs of the society that created them. A language develops and grows by constantly borrowing and making its own words and expressions from other languages and enriching its vocabulary. The idea that a language, complete in all respects, was created through the 'hand of god' is as absurd as the notion of an all-encompassing, ancient culture that has been handed down from generation to generation, frozen in time. The moment a language or a culture begins to resist change it begins to wither and fade.

Languages do not only transform over time, they also exist in different incarnations simultaneously within a specified region. A language gradually changes as one moves away from the core area of one linguistic region to its periphery, (this periphery would also mark the periphery of another language) and then into the core area of another linguistic region. A popular saying in north India, with two variations—*kos kos par bhasha badle do kos par paani* (language changes every two miles and the taste of water every four miles) and *paanch kos par bhasha badle teen kos par paani* (language changes every ten miles and the taste of water every six miles)—refers to the ever changing flavour of language.

Take Haryana for example: it shares its western and southern borders with Punjab and Rajasthan, its eastern border is brought up by UP and a little stretch to the north is shared with Himachal Pradesh. The Haryanvi spoken in the state has so many different inflections that many of them sound quite different from the core area Haryanvi that has come to be represented as the standard Haryanvi.

Each language has these variations and each variation is as valid as the other versions that prevail in neighbouring areas simultaneously. Thus any attempt to privilege one version as authentic and the others as impure is fraught with danger. This is as true of Urdu and Hindi, primarily urban languages, as it is of Haryanvi or Braj, both primarily rural languages. Who is to decide which version of Braj is authentic? The one spoken at Mathura or the one spoken at Vrindavan, the one in use at Agra or the one in use at Barsana (the village associated with Radha) or the Braj of Bharatpur.

But in an area as small as Delhi should it not be possible to identify the language that defined that area. I am not sure. I hope to be able to show through this narration the events that led to the evolution of the language of Delhi and the changes it went through and that, like all living languages, it has constantly changed and transformed itself and continues to do so even today.

I believe that it is impossible and incorrect to study the evolution of a language as a stand alone phenomenon. One must see this evolution as part of a larger social process. The changes that led to the emergence of the language of Delhi have, therefore, to be seen as part of a wider process of historical and social change and transformation that gradually led to the emergence of the syncretic culture of Hindustan.

Traditional accounts of the evolution of the 'language of Delhi' suggest that the arrival of central Asian influences during the Sultanate period (1206–1526) provided the trigger for the evolution of this language and that it rose to eminence during the Mughal period. This theory assumes that the 'language of Delhi' was without roots in the Indian milieu. As opposed to this traditional belief about the beginnings of the language, recent work predates the initial impulse for its birth by almost 1600 years. My narration begins in those times.

In the vast area of the Indian subcontinent, many languages and dialects existed much before the 'arrival' of early Sanskrit with the Aryans. The advent of the Aryans, the subjugation of the indigenous populations, the undermining of their languages and culture and the gradual establishment of the Chaturvarnashram (the division of society in four classes, the Dwij or twice-born Brahmin, Kshatriya and Vaisya and the so called 'low born' Shudra), eventually led to the establishment of Sanskrit, the language of the rulers, in a position of pre-eminence over indigenous tongues.

Discourses whether of a spiritual or secular nature increasingly began to be conducted in Sanskrit. The social stratification put in place by the mechanism of the Chaturvarnashram denied to the 'low born' the privilege of accessing the 'language of the Dwij'. This state of affairs continued almost unchallenged till two Kshatriya princes chose to reject the principles of inequality based on birth and began to preach in Pali and Magadhi, the popular tongues of the people.

The preference for the popular language over Sanskrit by both Gautama Buddha and Mahavir Jain marks a major departure in the evolution of languages in the Indian subcontinent, especially in the north. The rapid expansion of these faiths was accompanied by the growing use of local languages and dialects for communicating their spiritual message.

A wide range of languages and dialects began to receive and adapt new expressions from other languages and dialects through the Bhikshus and Jain monks who either travelled vast distances carrying their message or set up monasteries and institutes of learning that attracted students and scholars from distant places. The adoption of the language of the common people secularized and democratized the communication of ideas and knowledge.

This rapid expansion of dialects and languages spoken by

the common people was further strengthened when Asoka spread his message of a just order and good governance through the languages spoken by the people. His edicts were carved upon rocks and stone pillars in Magadhi and other regional and local languages including Aramaic and Greek in the present-day Kabul and Qandhar regions.

Buddhism travelled far and wide and those seeking to learn of the new faith travelled long distances to centres of Buddhist learning. Along with them arrived traders, travellers, artisans, stone masons and others. They brought with them their own symbols, images, music and languages, to be adapted, transformed and absorbed into what was eventually to become the 'great Indian tradition'.

It is the intermingling of these diverse cultures that makes the sphinx appear on the rock carvings at Mahabalipuram while Bactrian two-humped camels and Babylonian and Mesopotamian winged lions and goats find prominent representation at Sanchi.

Over the next few centuries this process of appropriation and fusion also left its imprint on indigenous cultural practices, visual, vocal, aural and textual which eventually (by the sixth century AD) saw the emergence of what the elite of the times called 'the apabhransas'—fallen languages. Shurseni the most widespread of the apabhransas of the north had by the late tenth century AD branched off into Braj, Awadhi, Khadi Boli, Maithili, Haryanvi, Punjabi, Marwari, Gujarati and a host of other languages and dialects.

The process of intermixing of people on both sides of the Khyber that had been going on since the arrival of the early Aryans and had continued with the influx of Greeks, Mongols, and others received a new input towards the close of the twelfth century. People seeking to make a home in Hindustan now began to outnumber the seekers of easy riches.

The spinning wheel and the Persian wheel arrived in the subcontinent as did new utensils and cooking styles, a different kind of music, new scripts and literary forms all of which combined with their local counterparts to create a new synthesis of life, language and culture. Trade between the Arabs, Turks, Afghans, Persians and local merchants prospered through the thirteenth and fourteenth centuries AD. Large sarais (inns) sprang up on the more popular trade routes and the saraiwala (the inn-keeper) began to communicate with his clients in a language that combined Punjabi, Khadi Boli, Sindhi, other local languages and dialects with expressions and phrases borrowed from Persian, Turkish, Arabic and Pashto. The result was the birth of a language that is today known as Saraiki (the language of the inn).

Little, if any, written examples of the Saraiki of those times survive. What we do have are some Saraiki verses ascribed to Bulleh Shah and Saraiki verses of Sachal Sarmast and Ghulam Fareed written in the eighteenth century. The credit for popularising the Saraiki poetry of Ghulam Fareed goes largely to the late Pathane Khan and one of the verses written by Ghulam Fareed and sung by Pathane Khan is reproduced below to give a flavour of the language:

Menda ishq vi tun, menda yaar vi tun,
Menda deen vi tun, imaan vi tun
Menda jism vi tun, menda ruh vi tun,
Menda qalb vi tun, jind jaan vi tun,
Menda Kaa'ba, Qibla, Masjid, Mimbar, Mushaf te Qur'an vi tun
Menda ishq vi tun, menda yaar vi tun

You are my love and my friend
My creed and my faith
My body and my soul
My heart and my life
You are my Kaa'ba, the Path of my prayers, my Mosque, my Pulpit, my Scriptures, my Qur'an
You are my love and my friend

Except for 'jind'—life, spirit, etc. in Punjabi—all the other attributes of the beloved/god are drawn from Arabic and

Persian while the grammar and usage is Saraiki, Sindhi, Multani. The text was easily understood across large parts of the north Indian plains.

As large armies owing allegiance to this or that aspirant to the Delhi throne engaged each other in battle and tens of thousands of local peasants became soldiers overnight another 'Creole' began to emerge. The officers spoke Persian, Pashto, Turkish and a range of Central Asian dialects and languages and the need to communicate orders and have them understood correctly and quickly, amidst the din of metal against metal and the thunder of galloping horses, gave birth to Lashkari, the language of the lashkar—the army camp.

Lashkari made use of a large number of words from Persian, Pashto, Turkish and other Central Asian languages. These words were absorbed, adapted and transformed by the peasant soldiers and travelled with them to far off villages as the armies dispersed after each campaign. Words like 'sipahi', that became sepoy in colonial English, have their origin in sepah—army in Persian. 'Bandooq', 'sandooq' and 'bandobast', terms for the gun, the trunk and arrangement, in common use in large parts of India are of Central Asian extraction. The Chahaar Bait—four line stanza that is sung to this day by the Rohelkhandi Pathans of west UP—was introduced by the Persian or Pashto speaking soldiers. These soldiers would gather around fires after a hard day of fighting to compose and sing Chahaar Baits about their valour in battle or about the beautiful girls that waited for them back home.

Al'a-ud-Din Khilji (1296–1316) used to give away tens of thousands of Khil'at and Jubba-o-Dastaar (gowns, caps, head gear and other garments) to those who had done well in battle or had fulfilled their duties diligently. He also gifted such raiment to his courtiers, high officials and envoys. Hundreds of master tailors, embroiderers and others were employed in a large number of kaarkhanas (workshops) in Delhi to ensure that the royal stores were well stocked with these garments at all times. Terms like zari (gold work), zardozi (gold thread embroidery), kasheeda kaari (embroidery), kaaftan (long gown-like coat), jubba, dastaar etc. found their way into daily usage through these artisans just as sangtarash (stone carver) became the commonly used designation for the stone masons that carried out repairs on the Qutub during the reign of Firoze Tughlaq in the mid fourteenth century AD.

Several small and large kingdoms had emerged by the thirteenth and fourteenth centuries. The victorious sardars and sultans began to build monumental structures in their newly established capitals. As artisans drawn from all over the subcontinent began working with the architects and designers who had accompanied the new rulers, their languages began to mix and many technical terms from both traditions intermingled to create a new vocabulary both in architecture and for the tools of the architect and the artisan.

Amidst marching armies, haggling traders and hectic construction activity there existed a silent, unobtrusive but fast growing presence, the Sufis. Within the short span of 600 years (from the twelfth to the eighteenth century) four major Sufi silsilas (traditions or schools)—the Chishti, the Qadris, the Suhrawardi and the Naqahbandi—left an abiding imprint on the spiritual and cultural life of the subcontinent. Though the Chishti tradition, introduced to India by Khwaja Moin-ud-Din Chishti, in the twelfth century, grew to be the most influential, there were many other illustrious Sufis such as the famous Suhrawardi Sufi Shams-ul-Arefeen Khwaja Turkman Bayaabaani, who made Delhi their base. In fact, Delhi came to be known as the abode of Sufi saints with more than a score prominent Sufis taking up residence in the city over the next few centuries. Three of the first five holy men belonging to the Chishti tradition, namely the second, Qutub-ud-Din Bakhtiyar Kaaki, the fourth, Nizam-ud-Din Auliya and the fifth, Naseer-ud-Din Chiraagh-e-Dehli settled in different parts of the city.

The Sufis kept their doors open to all creeds and castes and the ruler and the beggar turned to them for solace and guidance, in matters both profane and divine. Sufi shrines became centres for lively discourses, ecstatic music and passionate poetry. This culture of open-mindedness and tolerance produced some of the finest literature and music of the medieval period. The Sufis were in constant communication with the Bhakti poets, especially the Nirgunis—the worshippers of a formless, tolerant God. Both rejected orthodoxy and elaborate rituals and sought to communicate their simple but profound ideas to their unlettered followers in their own tongues.

Daadoo Dayal, the sixteenth century Nirguni says:

Jor na kare, haraam na khaaye
So momin bahisht mein jaaye[2]

The one who does not (oppress) use force
And does not consume things that are
impure and prohibited
Is a momin (believer) and will go to heaven

Note the use of 'jor', (zor in Persian for force), 'haraam'—impure/prohibited, 'momin'—believer and 'bahisht'—heaven. Dadoo wrote in Braj, the language that is spoken around Delhi in the region between Agra, Mathura and Bharatpur. A large number of Persian, Arabic and Turkish words were already a part of the vocabulary of the artisans of this region and Daadoo was an artisan, a cotton carder.

A common language, drawing upon diverse cultural resources began to develop in the Sufi shrines and akhadaas. This new language acquired its vocabulary and grammar from Khadi Boli and, as mentioned before, borrowed liberally from Persian, Turkish and Arabic and from local dialects. The language was Hindavi—also known as Zaban-e-Dehli or simply Dehlavi.

Nizam-ud-Din Auliya, the disciple of Baba Fareed, instructed his beloved disciple, the multi-faceted genius Amir Khusrau, to compose his poetry in Hindavi to facilitate better communication of Sufi ideas among the people. The songs that Khusrau wrote in praise of his preceptor, Nizam-ud-Din Auliya and the qawwalis ascribed to him use a mix of several languages notably Braj, Awadhi and Khadi Boli.

The following riddle with a spiritual twist, ascribed to Khusrau, is a fine example of this fusion:

Bakhat bakhat moe wa ki aas
Raat dina oo rahat mo paas
Mere man ko sab karat hai kaam
Ai sakhi saajan, na sakhi Raam[3]

I am restless without him
He is by my side day and night
He fulfils all my wishes
Is he your beloved? No my friend, He is GOD!

Note the colloquial use of bakhat for 'waqt' (Persian for time), 'dina' is Haryanvi and Braj for din (day), 'karat' is the verb 'to do' in Awadhi and Raam is used as a synonym for God and not necessarily for Ram the incarnation of Vishnu. This usage is common to Kabir, Nanak and many other Sufi and Bhakti poets as also in the much later writings of Mahatma Gandhi.

The qawwalis, riddles, proverbs and songs of the seasons that Khusrau composed in Hindavi became as popular as the poetry of Kabir. A prolific writer in Persian, Khusrau authored masnavis (a tale in verse, normally heroic, inspirational or reformist, a form that arrived in India from Central Asia), historical accounts, anthologies and treatises on music. Khusrau, who called himself Turk-e-Hindi (Turk from Hindustan), epitomized the coming together of the Central Asian and Hindustani traditions and their merging into a seamless whole.

The Sufi message spread rapidly from the environs of Delhi through Hindavi. Baba Fareed, the disciple of Bakhtyar Kaaki, took the language to Punjab in the thirteenth century. His poetry was later included in the Guru Granth Saheb.

Khwaja Banda Nawaz Gesu Daraz, from the same tradition moved to present-day Karnataka in the late fourteenth century and a centre for Hindavi and of Sufi thought developed around him at Gulbarga.

While the Sufis reached out to the people, the Sultans were busy capturing new territories. Both contributed to the spread of Hindavi. Al'a-ud-din Khilji captured Gujarat in 1297 and, in 1327, Mohammad Bin Tughlaq, ordered the entire population of Delhi to move to his new capital Deogiri in the Deccan and Hindavi acquired another foothold or two, south of the Vindhyas.

The Deccan prospered while Delhi, invaded by Taimur the Lame in the late fourteenth century, ceased to be the capital for a couple of hundred years. Taking advantage of these unsettled conditions, the Sardars of the Sultanate, both in the Deccan and Gujarat, revolted and set up independent kingdoms.

The breaking away of the Deccan and of Gujarat from the Delhi Sultanate and the formation of the Bahmani kingdom in the Deccan and the Ahmad Shahi kingdom in Gujarat proved to be of decisive importance for the growth of a language that was to return to Delhi 300 years later.

Both the Bahmani and the Ahmad Shahi kingdoms exchanged writers and scholars, adopted regional tongues and traditions and in a final break from Delhi and began to replace Persian with their own young languages. The adoption of languages other than Persian, the official language of Delhi, by these kingdoms was an act of defiance.

There was an exodus of writers and poets from Delhi to the more secure Deccan and Gujarat began. Patronised by the new kingdoms, Hindavi, Braj and Khadi Boli gradually fused into Telugu, Marathi, Gujarati and other local dialects and languages to emerge as Deccani and Gujari—languages in their own right—by the end of the sixteenth century. The 200 years from the fourteenth to the sixteenth centuries were crucial for the development of Deccani. Some of the most significant genres of poetic expression like the Masnavi and the Marsia (the Elegy recalling the Battle of Karbala) developed in the Deccan. The Deccani rulers of the Bahmani kingdom and its successors the Adil Shahi and Qutub Shahi poet kings of Bijapur and Golconda were great patrons of this language that was being transformed from Zaban-e-Dehli or Hindavi into Deccani.

The absorption and adaptation of a large body of new words and expressions from Marathi, Gujarati, Telugu and Kannada helped Deccani acquire a more expressive style with its own diction, forms of poetic expression and a body of work that included the first writings in literary prose.

Shortly after Tamerlane's repeated attacks on Delhi, the capital shifted to Agra and except for short spells during the time of Humayun and Sher Shah Sur, the capital continued to be located at Agra during the period of the Lodis (1451–1526) and three of the first four of the Mughal kings—Babar, Akbar and Jahangir. Agra was the heartland of Braj and Akbar patronized the language. He commissioned a large number of translations from Persian into Braj and the other way round. Faizi, one of his navaratans who was a great scholar of Persian and Braj was chosen to teach the language to Akbar's son Prince Danyal.

Eminent poets like Raskhan, Surdas and Mirabai chose Braj as their medium of expression. Mira like many of her precursors and contemporaries wrote in several languages. Afzal Panipati a contemporary of Jahangir wrote *Bikat Kahani*, a ballad in the Persian/Urdu script, in a language close to Rekhta / Khadi Boli that made free use of expressions from Braj. Awadhi too was established as a major language through the writings of Kabir, Malik Mohammad Jaisi in his *Padmavat* (written in the Persian/Urdu script) and later by Goswami Tulsidas in his magnum opus *Ramcharit Manas*. Words, phrases, expressions from Braj, Awadhi and other dialects and languages began to impact on Hindavi/Zaban-e-Dehli and were in turn influenced by it.

By the late sixteenth century this mutual give and take, between the languages of the subcontinent and those of

Central Asia, had become an established trend. The following couplet from Tulsidas testifies to this:

Tulsi sarnaam ghulaam hai Raam ko, ja ko rache so kahe kuchch o'uo
Maang ke khaibo, maseet ko soeebo, lebe ko ek na debe ko do'uo[4]

Tulsi is the slave of Raam, the creator, and cares not for anyone else
He will beg for food and sleep in a mosque, for he is beholden to none but God

Note the use of the word ghulaam—slave in Arabic and Persian—and the colloquialism of maseet for masjid (mosque).

The patronage given to Braj continued at the Mughal court even after the capital shifted to Delhi, at least up to the time of Aurangzeb, who himself wrote love poetry in Braj. Systematic works on the compilation of Rekhta/Urdu vocabulary were initiated during and after Aurangzeb's time and several dictionaries such as *Nawadir-ul-Alfaz* by Sirajuddin Ali Khan Aarzoo (1686–1756) were compiled.

Even when Delhi was no longer the capital during the late Lodi and early Mughal period Hindavi or Dehlavi continued to grow and develop in the large number of urban and semi-urban settlements that by now dotted the Delhi plains—Mehrauli, Begumpur, Hauz Rani, Adhchini, Chiragh-e-Dehli, Munirka, Zamarrudpur, Nizam-ud-Din and others.

The capital shifted back to Delhi with Shahjahan building a new city, Shahjahanabad. Persian was the officially patronized literary language, but in the narrow lanes and by-lanes of Shahjahanabad Zaban-e-Dehli or a language that later came to be known as Urdu emerged as the lingua franca. Though considered unfit for poetic expression by the Persian-speaking elite, Rekhta became the commonly spoken language in the city.

It was during this time that Wali's poetry arrived in Delhi

and shook the high brow world of Persian poetry. In his poetic expression, Wali broke the constricting grip of the tavern, the beloved and the wine bearer, and explored other human experiences including love for a city or a region.

Gujarat ke firaq soon hai khar khar dil
Betaab hai seene mane aatish bahar dil[5]

I miss Gujarat, thorn of memories pierce my breast
The heart is on fire and tries to break free of its bonds

Wali's simple style made the ghazal accessible to people outside the court. Arzoo, Abroo, Hatim, Bedil—all great poets of the Persian language—began to acknowledge the strengths of Dakkani, the language of Wali, now known increasingly as Rekhta. Rekhta had now become acceptable among the literati as a language capable of subtle expression.

The wide reach of Rekhta meant that wordsmiths from the plebeian ranks could now join the great masters. Rekhta had democratised the creative process. This was a major leap for a language that had grown in the battlefields, in the marketplace among haggling traders in caravan serais and in the shrines of the Sufis. The language continued to be spoken in the streets and by-lanes of scores of cities and towns in large parts of the subcontinent. Rekhta or Urdu, as the language was gradually beginning to be known as, was now firmly established as the language of Delhi.

The term Urdu has its origins in the Turkish word Ordu—army camp. The market where the soldier went to buy his daily needs came to be called the 'Urdu bazaar'. The open ground where the soldiers camped next to the Jama Masjid was known as 'Urdu maidan', and the Red Fort, the camp of the Supreme Commander, was the Urdu-e-Mualla.

The rise of Urdu coincided with the collapse of the Mughal Empire. Shah Alam II (1728–1806), who used the pen name 'Aftaab' is, in fact, the first Mughal ruler to have authored an anthology of Urdu poetry. It was during the early eighteenth century and thereafter that the language of Delhi spread and increasingly began to be patronized by the new kingdoms that came up as a result of the breaking up of the Mughal empire. Awadh, Bhopal, Rampur, and several other kingdoms, big and small, became new centres of Urdu.

As the language gained in popularity, it became the medium through which other disciplines were taught. The British, a growing presence from the mid eighteenth century, had gradually acquired a foothold inside the palace and were running the affairs of the city after defeating the Marathas and reducing Shah Alam to the status of a pensioner by 1803. The British had ambitions of taking over the administration and many senior British officers had begun to learn Persian, the language of the Mughal Court, in order to take over the moment an opportunity presented itself.

It was John Borthwick Gilchrist (1759–1841) who, after his travels across India from Gujarat to Bengal, advised the British to forget Persian, the language of the elite, and learn what he called Hindustani, the language that was spoken and understood across the subcontinent by the general population. Gilchrist compiled a dictionary of Hindustani, wrote several books on the grammar and usage of the language and later became the first President of Fort Williams College in Calcutta.

Gilchrist designed language courses for the officers in the East India Company and set up the first translation bureau at the college. The translation bureau did remarkable work in providing texts on diverse subjects to the people. The college initiated the policy of making two sets of translations, one in Urdu in the Persian script for 'Mohammedans' and the other in Hindi in the Devanagri script for 'Hindoos'. It was Gilchrist who gave the name 'Hindoostaani' to the spoken language of the region and it was Gilchrist who hired separate translators for the two scripts. Lashkari or Urdu, Hindavi, Zaban-e-Dehli, Deccani or Rekhta, call it what you will, had now split to become Hindi and Urdu: one for the 'Hindoos' and the other for the 'Mohammedans'.

This act of Gilchrist eventually created the idea of two separate cultures, for language and culture are joined by an umbilical cord and thus were 'created', a 'Hindoo culture' and a 'Mohammedan culture'. The two languages, two cultures, two peoples construct was to eventually contribute to the two nation theory, the Partition of India and the creation of Pakistan.

The swift rise to eminence of Urdu/Hindustani was facilitated by some outstanding poets, writers, lexicographers, essayists and critics that appeared on the literary scene in Delhi and its environs during the eighteenth and nineteenth centuries. The leading lights of this renaissance were Meer, Sauda, Dard, Ghalib, Momin, Zauq, Daagh, Mushafi, Insha, Sir Syed Ahmad, Nazeer Ahmad, Zaka Ullah, Altaf Husain Hali, Shibli Naumani and Meer Amman Dehlavi among others.

Education, both traditional and modern, now made rapid strides and the medium was Urdu. The Madrasa Ghaziuddin, started in 1703, was converted into Delhi College in 1825 and two of its faculty members Maulvi Zaka Ullah and Nazeer Ahmad were asked to translate the penal code into Urdu. Urdu became the official language of the courts in 1835.

Urdu was also the language of the 'rebellion of 1857'. Bahadur Shah Zafar, chosen as their leader by the rebel soldiers, issued a proclamation appealing to the people of Delhi to remain united in their resistance to the British. The proclamation was the first royal decree issued in Urdu. Bakht Khan, the commander of the rebel soldiers, drafted a constitution that was to govern the city once the British were removed from power. This constitution proposing the formation of an elected governing council was written in Urdu.

Delhi College, the Firangi Mahal Lucknow (a centre of Islamic learning that was started at the time of Aurangzeb in a palatial building earlier owned by a 'firangi', a French trader. The Translation Bureau at Hyderabad and the *Tehzeeb-ul-Ikhlaq* (a reformist educational magazine brought out by Sir Syed Ahmad Khan) initiated a movement to translate and write a large number of textbooks to introduce modern and scientific ideas in education in large parts of the country, especially north India.

During the next hundred years, Zaban-e-Dehli rose to become the language of intellectual discourse not only in the land of its birth but also in the Punjab, the Central Provinces, the United Provinces, in Bihar, in Hyderabad and many other places of undivided India. It became the vehicle for the articulation of the ideas of freedom and the creation of a just and free society. Those who gave voice to these ideas included Iqbal, Josh, Firaq, Faiz, Sahir, Majrooh, Majaz, Jazbi, Kaifi, Ismat, Bedi, Krishan Chander, Manto, Qurratulain Hyder, Jeelani Bano, Ram Lal and scores of others.

The events of 1947 displaced in one callous stroke a large population of Urdu speakers, who happened to be Muslims, from Delhi and many other cities and replaced them with those who spoke Punjabi and happened to be Hindus and Sikhs. The reverse happened in the newly formed Pakistan.

Pakistan, where Urdu was the mother tongue only of those who were forced to flee India, chose to make Urdu its national language. Hindi written in Devnagri became the official language of Bharat. This decision flew in the face of the express desire of the Mahatma that Hindustani written in both the Persian and Devnagri scripts should be the official language of a secular India. The decision in favour of Hindi came on the strength of the casting vote of the president of the session of the constituent assembly that had to decide the issue of the official language.

But languages that continue to absorb new influences, words, expressions and phrases cannot be decreed out of existence. The language of Delhi and its variants that had by the end of the nineteenth century become the language of Lucknow, Bhopal, Rampur, Patna, Gulbarga, Hyderabad and hundreds of cities across the subcontinent had also become the language of theatre, Hindustani cinema and of popular music. Its syncretism continues to enthral the connoisseur and layman alike through the ghazal, the qawwali and the film song.

Almost nine centuries ago, words like ghulaam, maalik, saheb, shalwaar, qameez, agar, magar, chunache, kyonke, baad, jaldi, ghalat, sahi, bistar, charkha, mez,[6] and thousands of others from Arabic, Turkish, Persian and Pushto had fused into Hindavi to create a language that came to be known as Urdu. During the last 300 years, too, the process of appropriating from other languages and traditions has continued to help this language to constantly reinvent itself and today the language of Delhi is fast developing into another Creole. Words like idea, style, house, hospital, bisicle (bicycle), pension, file, office, car and thousands of others have been incorporated into the vocabulary of the language of Delhi. The reverse process is evident in the inclusion of thousands of Urdu/Hindi words into English.

This process of assimilation continues at two levels. Words from other languages are appropriated, as they are, to be used in their original sense. This happens primarily with words that describe innovations that have no parallel in the tradition that is appropriating these words. Examples of this include words such as rocket, pressure cooker, motor car, thermometer, television and computer, etc. The other level of appropriation is to take a word or a term and to transform it in such a way that it comes to have a new life and meaning. The best example is perhaps fultroo (a meaningless appendage). The word 'fultroo' is a corruption of pull-through. The pull-through was a felt tipped steel rod that was used to clean the barrel of front-loaded rifles. Its transformation into fultroo is a stroke of sheer genius.

And so the chowkidar has become a guard, the madrasa is now a school, the mulazim has become a servant, the aayah has given way to a maid and mulazimat has become a job, shamianas have been replaced by tents, and the charpoy has turned into a bed while the Delhiwallahs carry a suitcase instead of a sandooq when they travel.

This is how languages have always developed and that is how they will continue to do so. Despite changes, languages manage to retain their individual flavour and the flavour of

Zaban-e-Dehli continues to inspire poets, writers and the lay person alike. Even today among the preferred qualities of the beloved in Bollywood cinema is the ability to speak in the language of Delhi:

> *Wo yaar hai jo khushbu ki tarah, hai jiski zaban urdu ki tarah*
>
> My beloved is like fragrance, her speech is akin to Urdu.

Notes

1 Jamil Jalbi, *Tareekh-e-Adab-e-Urdu* (Delhi, 1993), 1:7.
2 Syed Asad Ali, Hindi Adab Ke Bhakti Kaal Par Muslim Saqafat Ke Asraat, p. 57; Urdu translation by Majida Asad (New Delhi, 1991).
3 Mujib Rizvi, *Khusrau Nama*, (New Delhi, 1987).
4 Syed Asad Ali, Hindi Adab Ke Bhakti Kaal Par Muslim Saqafat Ke Asraat, p. 47.
5 Muhi-ud-Din Qari 'Zor', Daccani Adab Ki Tareekh (Aligarh, 1995), p. 108.
6 Slave, master, gentleman, salwaar, shirt, if, but, therefore, because, later, quick, wrong, right, bedspread, spinning wheel, table.

Dunu Roy

City Makers and City Breakers

Who makes cities? And who breaks them? These questions are relevant as all cities go through a phase of 'renewal'. In India this renewal is through the ambitious Jawaharlal Nehru Mission that has allotted over 150,000 crore rupees for 63 million-plus cities for seven years from 2005 to 2012 for this task. The immediate response of most people would be that it is enlightened governments and rulers who make truly good cities, and that it is invaders, terrorists and impoverished migrants who break them. But an instinctive reaction is not necessarily an indicator of reality, it could be a result of a mixture of propaganda and history; perhaps the 'truth' could even lie elsewhere. For cities have their own organic logic of growth. Different interests compete to make the city the way they want it. Those who fail to discover this central truth eventually end up seeing only their own needs as central to the city, at the cost of those whose lives are hidden beneath the grime and dirt on which the city is built.

Nothing illustrates this better than the modern history of the city of Delhi, the area where, in the remote past, the Pandavas, mighty warriors who laid to waste entire kingdoms in the name of honour and duty, possibly built their Indraprastha on the banks of the Yamuna river. The architect of this capital, the first city planner, was, curiously enough, a 'demon' named Maya—a foretaste of how the breakers have to demonise the makers if they want to lay claim to the fortunes and acclaim of history.

Company Power

The visible structure of the city is always imposed upon its social foundations. For instance, when even a casual visitor looks up at the imposing walls of the forts built by the Tughlaqs and the Mughals, it could occur to him that these walls could not have been actually 'built' by the kings. There must have been masons and stonecutters, water carriers and sand loaders, mixers and helpers, woodcutters and carpenters, ironsmiths and potters, labouring men and women and donkeys by the thousands who did the actual work. So where, in the pages of history, did they all disappear? Why were their memories not kept alive in prose and poetry, even if their humble wooden homes did not survive the ravages of time as did the stone walls of their rulers? Some indication of an answer comes near the end of the eighteenth century, when the East India Company began making deep inroads into the territories of Mughal India, marking the beginnings of what has been called 'nationalist' history—an interpretation of history that depicts an enslaved 'nation' being exploited by a colonial power.

The armed force on which the English built their power necessitated the planning and construction of barracks and Company quarters near every large town. The confluence of the ancient Grand Trunk Road and the newly commissioned Bombay–Agra Road in the first half of the nineteenth century made Delhi a place of crucial military importance. The aftermath of the Mutiny of 1857 led to further enforcement of control and the area around the Red Fort was cleared of the civilian population to enable the military to assert its supremacy. But what was this civilian population near the fort and why did it pose a threat to the new rulers? And why was the civil administration moved in 1912 to a Secretariat that was built far away from the fort, next to the northern

Ridge (near Metcalfe House, built in 1835 to house the Governor General's agent at the Mughal Court), within the safer confines of the Civil Lines? Did it have anything to do with distancing the bonded labouring classes from the reigning centre?

Immediately after the Mutiny it was also suggested by the British military commanders led by James Outram that the entire Walled City of Shahjahanabad be razed to the ground, but fortunately there was not enough explosive available for this task. While the Civil Lines for British administrators who took over power in 1803 had been laid out to the north of the Walled City, the Viceregal Lodge (now Delhi University) with its protective barracks was built in 1920 at an even safer distance from the subjugated 'natives', across and to the north-west of the Ridge. The imperatives of colonial rule were also reflected in the formation of the Delhi Municipal Committee in 1874. In the next decade the Committee proposed the construction of a commercial square outside the Walled City to the north, clearing the space for a new commercial quarter between Lahori Gate and Sadar Bazar, to be developed as a profitable enterprise in the tradition of the East India Company. The close of the century also saw the intrusion of the railway line as it broke through the ramparts of the Red Fort and Shahjahanabad. This new mode of transport began displacing the old trade routes with their sarais, since it generally followed the same alignments. So who was breaking and who was making the city?

Empire and Exclusion

The railways continued their expansion in the beginning of the twentieth century and, in the process, the new planners pulled down the bastions of the Walled City and filled the city's protective ditches and canals. Thus, Delhi Sadar station was constructed between the old town and Sadar Bazar, disrupting the organic linkage between the two, while a Mercantile Boulevard was proposed between the Kabuli and Ajmeri Gates—now celebrated as the decadent red light district of the city! It did not take long for the rulers to notice that a second, but lower class, city was organically growing in Paharganj (hillside market), Sadar Bazar (central market), and Sabzi Mandi (vegetable market) across the railway tracks. This led to the appointment of an Assistant Commissioner in 1908 as Officer on Special Duty to 'plan the future expansion of Delhi on an orderly basis'. This officer promptly recommended the westward expansion of the city across the Ridge and the 'improvement' of the older areas. By 1912, the dream of an Imperial city at Delhi was transformed into reality and a Town Planning Committee was appointed for the purpose.

This Committee oversaw the acquisition of extensive areas in the southern basin for the construction of an Imperial New Delhi. The architects Baker and Lutyens thus located the new Viceregal Palace (now Rashtrapati Bhavan) on the imposing height of Raisina hill with the new city spread out at its feet, to physically emphasise the difference between the rulers and the subjugated. Huge acreages were laid aside for the bureaucracy and ruling elite with spacious avenues and parks dominating the landscape. In the process much of the earlier drainage system, which had taken the run-off from the Aravalis to the tombs and gardens of the earlier rulers, was destroyed to make way for a new regime of storm-water drains. The Committee also decided to completely demolish the remaining city wall 'to provide access of air to the congested area'. This displaced a large number of artisans and workmen who lived near the city wall. So the Committee assigned the Western Extension Area (WEA) for expansion, particularly for settling the 'poorer classes'—or those who served the city with their labour. The railway line to the old capital of Kolkata also provided the pretext for forcibly acquiring prime agricultural land in 1915 from farmers on the east bank of the Yamuna river.

We get a glimpse of how an exclusive city was beginning to emerge when for the first time, in 1924, the Harphool Singh slum clearance project was officially sanctioned to forcibly move the poor population to the WEA. But three years later, in 1927, it was reported that there was now a population of 15,000 displaced poor people in the WEA living 'in much discomfort owing to lack of services'. In other words, one slum had given way to another through a planned process of displacement. Consequently, a northern expansion was recommended, beyond Civil Lines and across the Grand Trunk Road, on the outskirts of the old Sabzi Mandi. In spite of this, the government had to agree to sanctioning 10 lakh rupees in 1930 for providing basic services such as water and sanitation in the WEA (although as much as 23 lakh were required). As part of the planned process of urban development, several new roads had also been built into the new areas and each one of these showed good financial returns. But in the absence of other facilities, civic conditions continued to deteriorate so much that, in 1936, an ICS officer was specially appointed to go into the question of 'congestion in Delhi' and suggest appropriate measures.

Urban Sprawl

The recommendations of this officer eventually formed the basis for a further expansion of the city towards the Agricultural Institute (Pusa) in the west with adjacent industrial areas next to the railways. For this purpose, the Najafgarh jheel had to be drained and this was accomplished by digging a cut through the northern tip of the Ridge. In tandem, the Western Yamuna canal was filled up to the Andha Mughal bridge across the Sahibi river (now reborn as the Najafgarh nala once the jheel had been drained) on the pretext that the waters provided breeding grounds for the dreaded mosquito. This also enabled an expansion into the north through the new colonies of Shaktinagar and Roshanara Extension. These colonies were specially meant for the working poor, who had been evicted from 'evil slum areas' (as designated by the ICS officer) of the Walled City (now no longer with walls). Other areas from where the poor were displaced during the late 1930s were the Mohtaj Khana (destitute home) next to Sabzi Mandi, Rehgarpura (leather workers' hamlet) in the WEA (now reborn as genteel Karol Bagh), and Kala Pahar (black mountain) near Sarai Rohilla. The lands they vacated were converted gradually into middle-class residential areas.

The 1941 census revealed that, in forty years, the population had more than doubled to 9.17 lakh. The next few years were politically tumultuous and there was little time for mundane matters like town planning. But, with the partition of the country in 1948, there was a mass exodus from across the border and 4.5 lakh refugees arrived almost overnight in Delhi. The Ministry of Rehabilitation was entrusted with the task of resettling this huge population and it accomplished this by setting up a circle of colonies around the periphery of the city, mostly within the boundary set by what is now Inner Ring Road. Most of these 'refugee' colonies can be recognized by the names of the national leaders after whom they were named—Laxmi Nagar, Naoroji Nagar, Patel Nagar, Sarojini Nagar, Ranjit Nagar, and so on. The displaced families with means were rehoused in these colonies while others were allotted (mainly illegally) the large number of houses abandoned by those who had moved to Pakistan. Abandoned and new shops and industrial plots were also liberally made available for the refugee traders and entrepreneurs to economically and socially rehabilitate themselves.

The Annual Report of the ministry for 1948 shows how expeditiously the work was accomplished. A loan of Rs 42,62,075 was sanctioned for refugees in that year, of which Rs 24,31,150 was disbursed; Rs 2,57,700 were given to 175 traders and shop keepers; Rs 28,200 to 17 medical practitioners and chemists, Rs 23,500 to persons starting small-scale industry, while 80 women got Rs 20,250 for the purchase of sewing machines. A loan of Rs 1,92,985 was given to refugee students and Rs 39,024 as free grants to school students up to August 1948. Relief was given to 1,280 handicapped persons. Small urban loans (to be payable in easy installments) not exceeding Rs 500 were advanced to refugees; for the fist year they were free of interest, and for the next two years interest was to be charged at 3.5 per cent. To individual business and private limited companies, loans of up to Rs 50,000, and to joint stock companies up to one lakh rupees were allowed. As many as 1800 refugees secured jobs through the employment exchange up to March 1952. It is estimated that these loans resulted in the settlement of about 3 lakh displaced persons. So massive was the investment that, by 1951, the ministry considered that its job was over, but the dole continued until 1961, by when over Rs 18 crore had been transferred in property, Rs 14 crore in cash payments, and Rs 5 crore in remissions of dues. [It should be noted that in 1949 land was selling at Rs 3 per square yard in Delhi!]

However, this huge 'planned' expansion had its corollary effect on the city. In 1955 there was an epidemic of jaundice in the elite core of the city, in areas such as Civil Lines and New Delhi, and 700 people died. In the subsequent investigation it was discovered that considerable amounts of untreated sewage from some of the newly constructed planned refugee colonies at the periphery of the Ring Road were being discharged into the Najafgarh nala, which, in turn, was releasing its load into the Yamuna just downstream of the pumping station at Wazirabad. The city's water supply source was thus contaminated, resulting in the spread of the epidemic. In response to the disaster the Ministry of Health immediately set up a Town Planning Organization (TPO) and a barrage was constructed across the river at Wazirabad to separate the nala discharge from the water intake. The TPO also produced an Interim General Plan in 1957 to improve sanitation in the city by further displacing the poorer quarters, markets, and enterprises from the centre to the periphery, which is a good example of how the breakers of a city assume the mantle of makers, and reality is subsumed by myth.

Imposing Order

In order to provide better administrative and financial support to the planning exercise, Delhi was declared a Union Territory in 1956 and the Delhi Development Authority (DDA) was constituted in 1957 by an Act of Parliament 'to check the haphazard and unplanned growth of Delhi . . . with its sprawling residential colonies, without proper layouts and without the conveniences of life, and to promote and secure the development of Delhi according to plan'. For the next three years the TPO, guided by experts from the Ford Foundation, developed a Master Plan for Delhi for twenty years and this was presented along with maps and charts for unprecedented 'public' discussion in 1960, eliciting over 600 objections and suggestions from (as documented in the final Plan itself) 'the public, cooperative house-building societies, associations of industrialists, local bodies, and various Ministries and Departments of the Government of India'. It is interesting that associations of the working poor did not appear in this list of what constitutes the 'public'. An ad-hoc Board was appointed to go into all these objections and it reportedly granted a personal hearing to all the objectors. Eventually the Master Plan of Delhi was formally sanctioned in 1962 and came to be known as MPD-62.

MPD-62 acknowledged that Delhi was likely to have an urban population of 56 lakh by 1981 unless measures were taken to restrict it to 50 lakh (without, of course, stating why an extra 6 lakh could not be accommodated—as had happened perforce in 1948). The planners proposed to do this by building a 0.6 km wide green belt around Delhi and diverting the surplus population to the seven ring towns in Uttar Pradesh and Haryana. In a repetition of colonial history, it was once again decided that the Walled City would be 'thinned out' by relocating the population to New Delhi and Civil Lines. In 1961 there were also estimated to be 8,000 industrial units, which were located in 'non-conforming' industrial areas such as Karol Bagh, Shahdara, Naraina, Malaviya Nagar, Kalkaji, Tilak Nagar etc. So, several new industrial areas were designated for accommodating these industries on 5800 acres. The plan also provided for 85 square yard plots with services for poorer families who were going to come to Delhi to work in these industrial areas and commercial centres to be set up in different zones. In the process the DDA became the sole developer of the largest nationalization of land in the world, outside the Communist nations.

But by 1971 it was becoming clear that the city was going to grow far beyond the calculations (but not the declared targets given in the Master Plan) of the planners. The number of industries had increased to 26,000 and there was a huge spurt in the squatter population of the urban working poor—although both these had been anticipated by the Master Plan. So, in a frenetic burst of activity, the administrative machinery swung into action and, from 1975 to 1977, 1.5 lakh squatter families, consisting of a total population of 8–9 lakh were forcibly moved out of the centre of the city into resettlement colonies on the periphery of the growing city. Each family was entitled to a plot of only 25 square yards with common services of water, electricity and sanitation, and 60,000 such plots were demarcated, mainly on the low-lying Yamuna flood plain to the east. Interestingly, all the colonies were located very near the new industrial areas, thus indirectly giving a clue about the working class character of the evicted population required for providing cheap wage labour. At the same time, in 1977, the government regularized 567 'unauthorized' colonies which had come up in contravention of the Master Plan, inhabited by a more white-collar population, so that they could now officially avail basic civic services that had been denied them earlier because they were unauthorized.

Modifying Plans

A new Master Plan should have been ready by 1982. But, instead, the entire city was geared to host the Asian Games that year. Numerous roads, hotels, flyovers, offices, apartments, and colonies were constructed to cater to the needs of the Games and the anticipated commercial spillover. The second Outer Ring Road became a magnet for further commercial and residential development. So while one work force was moved out of the city during the 1975–77 period to make space for the infrastructure required for the Games, another had to be summoned for building the new infrastructure between 1979 and 1982. It is estimated that 10 lakh workers came to Delhi during this period alone. But the city fathers claimed that they could not cope with this additional 'burden'. In 1985, the National Capital Region Board was set up in an attempt to plan for the balanced growth of the extended region around the capital where this 'surplus' population would be accommodated.

Also in 1985, the first draft of the second Master Plan was published for comments. However, unlike the first Plan, this one was not summarized or translated into Hindi and Urdu, nor was it distributed publicly. Nevertheless, the draft came in for severe criticism from the government itself as being 'conceptually defective' and the Delhi Urban Arts Commission (DUAC) was asked to prepare another plan. DUAC took a close look at the failures of the first Master Plan to detail its own Conceptual Plan. It was discussed in a select committee and modified to yield the second Master Plan, known as DMP-2001. This plan, probably recognizing the failure of the government to meet the targets set in MPD-62, lowered the bar and called for limiting the urban population (to 112 lakh) by de-industrialization (in other words, rendering the labouring classes redundant), though it had nothing to offer for the non-conforming industrial units already existing (then estimated at 24,000). Thus, on one hand the authorities grudgingly acknowledged the contribution of the working poor in making the city, but on the other hand the planners persisted in deliberately breaking their livelihoods and shelter. Interestingly, DMP-2001 displayed the modern planners' inherent ignorance of indigenous planning when it called for a 'special area' status for the Walled City as 'it cannot be developed on the basis of normal planning policies and controls'.

Two years after the sanction of the new Plan, in 1988, there was an outbreak of cholera reminiscent of the 1955 jaundice epidemic. This time, 1500 people died and they were all from the 44 resettlement colonies that had been constructed during 1975–77 and the 625 slum clusters where the working poor lived. These included areas like Gautampuri, Seelampur, Nand Nagari, Kalyanpuri, Dakshinpuri, and Mongolpuri. Unlike in 1955, however, there was no concerted response from the administration. Even the disbursement of compensation (which had been laid down as part of procedure during the jaundice epidemic of 1955) was withdrawn, though it was recognized that the disease had spread through ground water contaminated due to inadequate sanitation measures. This was inevitable given the nature of the low-lying areas in which the resettlement colonies had been located, by plan, in the first place. Thus, DMP-2001 was not only unable to tackle the problems created by the earlier period, it did not even incorporate its own analysis of the failures and weaknesses of past planning in its recommendations.

City and Class

This systemic failure of planning is evident in the situation today, seven years after the target date (2001) when a new Master Plan should have been prepared, and one year after it was actually notified (2007). Delhi has spread far beyond the confines of the Outer Ring Road. The green belt, which was specified in MPD-62, has largely fallen victim to land developers. The resettlement colonies and industrial areas, that were supposed to be at the fringe of the city, have been drawn into its ambit. Narela, for instance, which was supposed to be a ring town under MPD-62, is now a connected suburb. Gurgaon, Faridabad, and Ghaziabad are contiguous urban sprawls and the arterial roads and national highways are the most congested in the region. And increasing numbers of the poor continue to live in shanty towns without services. In 2008 it was estimated that there were over 1500 unauthorized colonies without civic amenities, over 1100 slum clusters with minimal urban services, and as much as 60 per cent of the population lives in sub-standard housing because the civic authorities have been unable (or unwilling) to provide adequate space for the shelter and livelihoods of the very people who constitute the backbone of the city's economy. Once again, history as it unfolds repeats the question of who are the makers and who are the breakers of the city?

For such an ancient city, it is to be expected that history will provide some curious twists and lessons for the makers of the new city. But, as the vision of a world-class city rises over the social horizon, new history emerges to be even more formidable and gnarled than the old, as it refuses to acknowledge the presence of the working poor while catering only to the exclusivity of the elite. Even the courts appear to be colluding in this although their mandate is to preserve the balance between the classes. Thus, between 1994 and 2002, thirty manufacturers' and resident welfare associations filed writs in the Delhi High Court praying for the removal of slum encroachments from their areas, while thirty-six slum associations and individuals filed petitions asking for adequate housing. But, by November 2002, without giving any opportunity to the slum dwellers to be heard, the judges of the two Benches hearing the various cases, ordered the demolition of all slums as well as quashed the policy providing for resettlement of those who were evicted. In this manner, two judgements by two judges gave sweeping powers to the administration to uproot slum dwellers everywhere in the city.

Law and Justice

Subsequently, when one of the High Court judgements was temporarily stayed by the Supreme Court, that Bench on its own volition took up the issue of pollution of the Yamuna river and in March 2003 directed all concerned authorities 'to forthwith remove all the unauthorized structures, jhuggies, places of worship and/or any other structure which are unauthorizedly put (sic) in Yamuna Bed and its embankment'. But when the Uttar Pradesh Irrigation Department Employees Federation challenged the construction of the Akshardham temple on the same Yamuna riverbed, the Court held that the temple was an existing reality built at great cost, and dismissed the writ. And in January 2004, a series of ruthless demolitions of unauthorized constructions began all over the city. It may thus be seen that there is a systematic exclusion on the one hand and selective inclusion on the other, that masks the ideological divide between who creates and who destroys the structural fabric of the city and for what purpose.

This bifocal view continues unashamedly. At august gatherings of the elite, speakers wax eloquent about Singapore and Paris and Shanghai. Eminent industrialists hobnob with high profile television commentators, senior bureaucrats, and the city's beautiful people to announce the coming of the global, shining future. When the designer malls on MG Road were partially brought down in early 2006 there was a huge hue and cry. The sealing and demolition of about 1000 shops and commercial establishments in the next few months occupied centre stage in all the newspapers and the Government was forced to introduce a Bill in Parliament to put an end to these. But there was little or no concern in the media for the over 60,000 poor working families uprooted in three years in the name of 'beautification' for the world class city. Many of these families have been sent to remote sites like Bawana and Sabda Ghevra for so-called 'resettlement', where the stark non-availability of basic facilities like toilets and transport, water and electricity, employment and education, dispensaries and dustbins have been systematically documented by voluntary groups. But whenever evidence of these appalling conditions has been placed before the superior courts and human rights bodies, they have been arrogantly brushed aside.

What is concealed behind this play of history is that both sets of lives across the class barrier are affected by the failure of inclusive governance in the city. Thus, only one-third of the housing stock, one-fifth of the commercial space, one-third of the industrial area, and one-sixth of the informal sector space targets, as stipulated by DMP-2001, have actually been made available in the city in the last 25 years by agencies such as the DDA and the Municipal Corporation of Delhi. Hence, the unfortunate citizens, whether those wishing to operate shops and services, or those struggling to survive on an inhospitable piece of land, have had no other choice than to become 'illegal', 'unauthorized', and 'non-conforming'. Within the network of relationships that encompass the city, between employer and employee, between service provider and consumer, between those who toil and those who soil, the inclusion of one is inevitably affected by the exclusion of the other. But, instead of recognizing this interdependency and holding the agencies to task for their failure, the Courts have victimised those who have tried to create economically viable alternatives in housing and employment through their own enterprise and imagination.

In the meantime, the executive merrily continues to invest huge amounts of public money in projects like the Metro, the Commonwealth Games, and the vast residential and shopping complexes in the south and east of the city. Not only are these projects not part of the Master Plan, which is the only legal document governed by an Act of Parliament, but they have taken power away from the people's elected representatives and vested them in wholly arbitrary and publicly unaccountable bodies like the Delhi Metro Rail Corporation, the Commonwealth Games Committee, and the DDA. Not only are they, therefore, legally non-planned, they are also uneconomical. The Metro, for instance, on its own admission, in 2008 carried one-fifth of the passengers which it was supposed to carry when it was designed and was being subsidized to the tune of Rs 67 on every ticket it sold. Similarly, no modern Games in the last forty years has made a profit. In fact, for the last Commonwealth Games in Melbourne the cost climbed from an initial Aus$190 million to a staggering Aus$1.1 billion and the City Council estimates that it will take twenty years to pay back the public debt! Yet these projects are held to be models for the redevelopment of the city. Manifestly, a concept of 'law' that favours the powerful has replaced that of 'justice' that treats everyone as equal.

Dying Light

In effect, the rulers of the city have ignored the fundamental principles of science (what causes pollution?), justice (who is accountable?), and human rights (men and women are to be treated equally?) to deny the urban poor their entitlements while favouring the affluent. This has been further complicated by the fact that the Constitution recognizes only those persons as 'citizens' who either have a birth certificate or hold a title to property. In a country where the majority of births go undocumented and at least one-third of the population has no property, such a definition of citizenship is farcical. It completely disempowers those who labour for a living but have no papers to prove that they exist in the eyes of the law. It gives enormous leeway to the police, municipal, and sundry other officials to harass and extort from all those who have no written proof of citizenship. Instruments like the Foreigners Act, charges of vagrancy and beggary, of narcotics and theft, are freely used by these officials to torment those unfortunate enough to become dirty while keeping the city clean. This includes the entire gamut of what is called the 'informal sector', and the list is long and comprehensive.

As the capital moves in a completely discordant manner towards a tryst with the Commonwealth Games in 2010—reminiscent of the earlier tom-tomming of the Asian Games in 1982—and the city fathers (and mothers) posture in world-class fashion, the people of the city have artificial walls built around them. Hawkers and vendors can no longer ply their trade because they are held guilty of occupying the space of pedestrians (who have already been evicted by the motor-car), non-polluting cycle rickshaws are banned because they supposedly cause congestion, the migration of the domestic servant and service sector worker to the city is to be stopped because they are apparently responsible for the breakdown of civic facilities, and the urban space is to be protected for the mall, the flyover, the motorized vehicle, the skyscraper, and the gated colony.

Such walls and such worlds can only breed more violence as social interconnectedness is rent asunder and human beings are alienated from each other and from the organic city. And, once again, the rulers will blame the people for the violence while they shrug off all responsibility. But will the bricklayers and stonemasons vanish to suit the vision of the masters? What about the pullers and the loaders, the nannies and the drivers, the repairmen and saleswomen? What about the waste pickers and sewer cleaners, the delivery boys and tailoring girls, the factory workers and the artisans? Do they not make the city as well? And what do they get in return? Those who service the city get no services in exchange. And yet they are regarded as thieves and pickpockets, a burden on the city and creators of dirt. Over them hangs the perpetual threat of 'illegality' and 'demolition'. The real 'makers' are confronted by the surreal 'breakers': and all in the name of a clean environment and healthy sports and enjoyable tourism.

Simmer of Discontent

The pages of contemporary history are once again echoing an oft-repeated question—will the working poor go silently into the night? Or will they rage, rage against the dying of the light? Whatever evidence is coming, through the eyes of those involved in a dialogue with them, indicates that there is vast discontent brewing within the army of the dispossessed. The rag picker on the streets, the watchman outside the bungalow gates, the ayah who cleans and dusts and sweeps within, the driver and the electrician and the plumber and the mason who drift in and out between outer and inner spaces, watch how the rich play at both work and home. They hear the voices of arrogance that claim the city for their own. And when they return to their homes in the midst of squalor and want, they also know that Delhi is being transformed into Paris.

On one side there are the visual and audio images of Radio

Mirchi; the gleam of shop windows and ice-cream parlours; the sophisticated voices of *bhav* and *sanskriti*; the smug seminar satisfaction of 'problem-identified, problem-tackled, problem-solved'; the seductive calls to drink more water for healthy skins; the invocation of Las Vegas and Singapore and Sydney as the icons for modernity; and the vacuous assertions of the cheer-leaders that 'we can do it'. On the other side are the slapping sounds of naked feet on the road pulling cartloads of goods; nimble fingers deftly cooking rotis for shrinking bellies; the struggle to get children into petty government schools where they will be called offspring of *bhangis*; the daily search for shreds of dignity within the violence of the public latrines, the packed buses, and the policed streets.

In between there is also the pause for reflection; the nagging question—is this the city we really want? But, curiously enough, this pause finds no space in the conference halls of the effete. The captains of industry and commerce, the suave TV anchor, the omnipotent bureaucrat-administrator, the hip-hop college student, the outstanding engineer, are all convinced of their place in destiny as the makers of the future. But for that they have to inevitably break the past—and, often, the present too. So as the Metro glides through the city the commuters are unaware of the huge cost the city is paying for this symbol of modernity, and of the thousands whose homes and livelihoods were removed to make way for the steel rails. The sportsmen and tourists who will stream into the city in 2010 will not be told that their games are to be played on the graveyards of labourers who constructed the stadia and hotels and were then banished into the wilderness. And as Nehru's visage ponders on the coins and Gandhi's smiles out of currency notes, the development that takes place in their names is critically challenged only by those whose misfortune it is to build homes for others while their own are razed to the ground.

Interstitial Hope

Perhaps it is in the interstices of this dialectic that hope lies for the future? There is the profound Supreme Court judge who declares in 2000 from the leafy enclaves of Lutyens' Delhi that the jhuggi-dweller is a land-grabber and pronounces, 'Rewarding an encroacher on public land with free alternate site is like giving a reward to a pickpocket'. And there is the irate office-boy standing before his demolished home asking, '*Saat hazar rupaiye lekar, barah gaz zameen dekar sarkaar hamare oopar ehsaan kar rahi hai kya?*' (Is the government doing us a favour by giving us twelve yards of land for Rs 7000?) There is the police inspector who visits the sordid resettlement colony of Bawana on behalf of the National Human Rights Commission and magnanimously reports, 'The concerned authorities are making efforts to provide basic amenities to the resettlers . . . Such large scale projects do have their own difficulties including delays in sanctions and resource crunch.' And there is the domestic maid who stirs her cooking pot to reflect, '*Dilli shaher? Hamara bhi shaher hai. Hum bhi apna haq lar kar le sakte hain.*' (Delhi city? It is our city too. We can also fight for our rights.)

The question is whom do we choose to believe? Do we trust those 6 lakh families who live in the *pucca* colonies of the city? Or do we listen to those voices from the 6 lakh families located in the jhuggis? What about the 7 lakh in the *kachhi* colonies? And the 4 lakh who have been forcibly moved from one arena of illegality into another to inhabit the resettlement areas? And do we completely forget the two lakh now condemned to inhabit the pavements because there is no affordable space for them anywhere? Every third human being in Delhi is part of the workforce, those who sustain the life of the city, and 80 per cent of them are in the informal sector. So whom do we believe? The officials of the Confederation of Indian Industry gloating over 8 per cent-plus growth, or the workman shading his eyes from the hot afternoon sun, '*Dilli mein mazdoor ke liye kuchh nahi hai, kuchh nahi hai*' (There is nothing in Delhi for the labourer, nothing)?

The way forward depends upon the choice we make. If we believe the property developer, the expert, the bureaucrat, the entrepreneur, and the politician, then we have placed our faith in those who are breaking the city but pretend to make it. If we open our minds to the sounds of the vegetable sellers and auto drivers, the brick-layers and beauty parlour assistants, the steel welders and sewer workers, the domestic *bais* and home-based *biri* producers, then we will hear the cadences of the actual makers of the city, but who are often accused of breaking it. Will the choice be made freely and democratically? Or will it eventually be made through the violence of another democracy being born on the streets? That too is a choice we may be forced to make—or break.

Priti Narain

Dilli Ka Asli Khana (The Real Cuisine of Delhi)

An Australian gentleman once asked my father which part of India he came from. On receiving the reply, 'Delhi' he expressed surprise and said, 'Surely you mean UP? How can anyone belong to Delhi?' My father explained that his ancestors had worked in the Mughal courts and that several generations of his family had lived in Delhi. The gentleman called his wife and said, 'Come and meet an aborigine of Delhi!'

What the Australian may not have known is that Delhi is a very old city whose origins are said to date back to the Mahabharata era. Tradition has it that the Pandavas built Indraprastha, the first of the cities that came to be known as Delhi. According to some sources this was as early as 1450 BC, but others place it anywhere between the tenth and eleventh centuries BC. In any event, since that time Delhi has stood at the crossroads of history. The city has been occupied, abandoned and rebuilt at different sites by various peoples through the ages. The Pandavas, the Rajputs, invaders from Central Asia, the Mughals and the British all made Delhi their capital. Buddhist monks from central India made their way through the city on their missions to northern parts of the country and to Asia, and European traders arriving on the Indian coastline found their way to Delhi.

Independence brought the people of the Punjab and subsequently others from different parts of India who also made their homes here. Thus Delhi became a melting pot of these varied traditions, customs and cuisines.

The early inhabitants of the city seemed to have enjoyed a fairly rich diet—there are references in the Mahabharata to dishes made with rice, ghee, milk, honey and roots. They also ate a variety of meats which included deer, sheep, pig, cow, fowl and even donkey and camel! Meat was cooked with rice and there were dishes which combined meat and fruit. Cooking methods included roasting meat on a spit, grinding boiled meat with spices and roasting it on skewers, much like today's kebabs, and cooking meat in spiced curries.

The influence of the pacifist tenets of the Buddhists and Jains from the sixth century BC saw a more austere diet evolve with a greater emphasis on vegetarianism. The priestly class began to shun meat and also dropped onions and garlic from the menu considering them to be foods that aroused base passions such as lust and anger. The Chinese pilgrim I Ching, who visited India between 671 and 695 AD, noted that onions were forbidden as they 'caused pain, ruined the eyesight and weakened the body'. To this day the Bania and Jain communities follow a strict vegetarian diet sans onion and garlic.

The Rajputs, who ruled Delhi between the seventh and tenth centuries AD, reintroduced meat, onions and garlic to the menu. The Central Asians, who began making forays into India from the tenth century, not only ate meat but also cooked in animal fat. Mahmud Ghazni raided India around 1000 AD and by 1206 AD, the Slave dynasty was established in Delhi, followed by the Khiljis and the Tughlaks. These early invaders brought the tandoor and also the nuts and raisins of their native lands. In India they found an abundance of cereals, pulses, vegetables, herbs and spices, and also ghee used as a cooking medium. By combining ingredients and cooking methods from their homeland with those found in India, the early Muslims played an important part in the creation of a cuisine that was unique to the subcontinent.

They also introduced the concept of community eating and a more formal dining etiquette. The indefatigable traveller, Ibn Batuta, who visited India between 1325 and 1354 AD, described at length the dining customs of the Delhi Sultans. He said there was a formal ritual for both private and public dinners. The private dinners were attended by the Sultan and had a formal seating arrangement where judges, orators and jurists were given places of honour, followed by the Sultan's relatives, nobles and finally the common people. A rose-flavoured sherbet was served when the guests were seated. The meal which followed consisted of meat cooked in ghee and flavoured with ginger and onion, naan, meat-filled samosas, rice, fowl and halwa. A barley drink and paan ended the meal. Paan had its own etiquette and was offered to welcome a guest as well as to bid farewell. At the public dinners too there was a formal seating arrangement. The Sultan was not present but the palace officers presided and in order of seniority made speeches in the ruler's honour. Only then did the dinner commence. Both Ibn Batuta and Amir Khusro (1253–1325 AD) gave detailed descriptions of the sumptuous fare enjoyed by the rich. An abundant quantity and variety of meats, rice, rotis and sweets were served at their lavish feasts, the leftover food being distributed to the poor. It may be mentioned here that most of the Sultans as well as the Mughals who followed them enjoyed wine.

With the coming of the Mughals in 1526 AD, there were further developments in the culinary sphere. Babar, who missed the melons and grapes of his native land, started their cultivation in India and by the time of Akbar there was a large range of fruit and vegetables available in the Delhi markets, grown locally as well as imported from Kandahar and Kabul and the coastal regions of India. The price lists in the *Ain-I-Akbari* mention a variety of vegetables and fruit including fennel, spinach, turnips, cabbage, oranges, Samarkand apples, pomegranates and pineapples. Jahangir in his memoirs says that pineapples came from the harbour towns held by the Portuguese and were called *kathal-i-safari* or 'travelling jackfruit', as young plants could be carried on journeys and would yield fruit.

The Mughals did not follow an exclusively meat-rich diet. According to contemporary accounts, Humayun would give up eating animal flesh for days and often months. He also declared that beef was unfit for the devout. Abu'l Fazl tells us that Akbar did not like meat and disapproved of the needless killing of animals. 'If his Majesty had not the burden of the world on his shoulders, he would at once totally abstain from meat.' As it was, Akbar did not eat meat on particular days and even months of the year. He started his meal with rice and curds and ate simple food out of choice. Jehangir also observed vegetarian days and forbade animal slaughter on Thursdays and Sundays. Aurangzeb, by all accounts, was a spartan who did not relish meat and subjected himself to numerous fasts. The Mughals also classified cooked food into three categories: the first was safiyana food, eaten during days of fasting and consisted of vegetables, rice, wheat, lentils, halva, and sweet sherbets. The second category included rice cooked with meat such as pulao and biryani, haleem and harisa which were a combination of wheat and meat cooked together. And the third was kebabs and rich meat curries with plenty of ghee and curds.

In the meantime, the Europeans had also discovered India in their quest for spices. The Portuguese were the first to arrive followed by the Dutch, the French and the British, and a lively trade developed between Europe and India. Cookery is not a static art but an evolutionary process where elements from different culinary disciplines are absorbed by and enrich each other. Thus the coming of the Europeans had a profound influence on the development of Indian cuisine. Ingredients such as potatoes, tomatoes and chillies, which are an integral part of Indian cookery today, came from foreign shores. The same is true of cauliflower, peas and beans. Although Indians used mildly leavened dough to make naan and khamiri roti, it was with the Europeans that 'double-roti' or fully leavened bread made an appearance. The innovative cooks of Delhi created the delicious shahi tukra using this foreign bread, fried and layered with sweet, thickened milk and nuts.

Delhi as we know it today began to take shape with the building of Shahjahanabad in the seventeenth century. The inhabitants of the city were Muslim, Bania, Jain, Kayasth and Khatri. The emperor had also brought in Kashmiri pandits who being proficient in Sanskrit, Arabic and Persian translated texts which helped to settle disputes regarding property and temple affairs. All these communities lived in harmony and interacted with one another, attending weddings and exchanging gifts at each others festivals. The affluent vied with each other to produce elaborate feasts with a large range of food on the menu.

Cookery books of the time suggest menus for special feasts where five varieties of each kind of food should be offered. For instance:

Pulaos could be chicken, fish, muzaafar, muthanjan or saffron biryani.

Kebabs were chicken, fish, partridge, quail or duck. (Kebab referred to dry roasted meat and not the tikka of today. It was called 'gazak' and was an accompaniment to alcohol or 'daaru').

Saalans were shabdeg, qorma, meat cooked with almonds, fried arvi or turnip.

Pakwan (fried breads) included plain and stuffed poories, samosas and gauja. In this category were also rotis, taftaan naan, bakarkhani, salty and sweet layered parathas and khaas birayi roti. Pickles, preserves and malai were served along with the meal. Sweet dishes included shahi tukra, gulatthi (rich kheer made with ghee and malai), phirni, lauz and jalebi. Ordinary feasts, of course, were much less elaborate.

The Muslim food that had evolved consisted of rich meat curries, biryanis and pulaos, cooked in liberal amounts of ghee and enriched with raisins, nuts and dried seeds of melon and pumpkin. Cooking techniques were quite sophisticated.

Seekh kebabs, large rotis and naan were made in a tandoor while smaller rotis were cooked on a tawa. For meat curries and qormas the traditional Indian round-bottomed pot with a narrow neck was used; very little or no water was added and long, slow cooking on a choolha ensured that the flavours of the spices blended with the meat and vegetables. Often the cooking pot was sealed with dough, a process that came to be known as dum pukht. Meat was also marinated in a mixture of spices and yoghurt prior to cooking. An interesting way to add a smoky flavour to a meat dish was 'dhungar'. This involved placing a live coal in a katori of ghee which was put on the meat. The pot was sealed and left for an hour or so for the smoke to permeate the meat, and the ghee was also mixed in. For pulao a richly flavoured meat stock was prepared and then rice and meat were cooked together in this; for biryani cooked or uncooked, marinated meat was combined with partially cooked rice and put on dum till done. Rice cooked with vegetables, usually peas, was and is called tahiri. Rice was also combined with dal, onions and spices to make khichree and often meat was also added. This elaborate dish, full of ghee, masala and raisins, was a far cry from the khichree that is served to invalids today. There were also curries combining mutton with lentils or different vegetables such as potato, turnip, ghia and also lotus seeds. Soaked and pounded wheat was also cooked with mutton to a porridge-like consistency to make harisa and haleem. The latter also had chane ki dal added to it.

Nahari, which is usually eaten at breakfast, has a story behind it: when Shahjahanabad was inaugurated in 1648 the festivities lasted ten days but the Shahi Hakim did not attend. When questioned about this lapse he is said to have replied that the water of the canal which ran through Chandni Chowk was extremely noxious and would be harmful for the populace. As Shah Jahan was not about to abandon his capital he asked for a remedy. The hakim recommended a diet rich in spices and fat. Although spices were plentiful the poor could not afford the large amounts of ghee recommended. The problem was solved by using trotters, which were otherwise discarded, adding some calf muscle and simmering it overnight. The following morning (nahar means morning) the nahari along with kulcha was distributed free to the poor to provide at least one substantial meal for the day. This custom has been continued by some well-to-do families to the present day. Another source says that it was Aurangzeb's Hakim Alvi who said that the canal waters were harmful and recommended the use of spices as an antidote and that this was the origin of Delhi's chaat. Perhaps both versions are correct.

Of the communities living in Shahjahanabad, the Kayasthas and Khatris worked in the Mughal courts and their language, culture and cuisine were greatly influenced by that of the Muslims. This was especially true of the Mathurs. They were (and still are) extremely fond of food and delighted in creating new recipes. Some famous dishes include shabdeg which is a combination of mutton kofta, kidneys, turnips and potatoes in a rich gravy, simmered overnight on charcoal embers, to which cooked brains are added before serving; bharvan parsinde where thin slices of mutton are beaten lightly and wrapped around a mixture of chopped onion, herbs and spices and cooked slowly in masala. There are as many recipes for raan or leg of mutton as there are cooks. My husband's family recipe involves marinating the meat for twenty-four hours, cooking without using any water, then adding ground roasted chana and spices. This fairly dry dish would keep for several days and could be carried on journeys. The Mathurs also developed vegetarian dishes to resemble mutton or liver. The humble lentil was soaked and ground and the resulting batter was used to make dal ki kaleji and dal ka keema. Koftas were made with any number of vegetables, and green bananas were turned into kele ke parsinde. Snacks to accompany drinks included bhunva kaleji, bhunva murgh and shami kebab.

An important factor in the development of the rich and varied cuisine of Delhi was the joint family which has long been a part of Indian society. With many hands available and each family having its own favourites, the women would spend a great deal of time and effort adapting recipes to create new and elaborate dishes. Often the men would throw in suggestions about trying different ingredients and combinations. But it was during festivals and weddings that the joint family really came into its own.

Among Mathurs, Khatris and Banias, wedding preparations began with the making of mangories by the women of the family. Tiny heaps of moong-dal pitthi (batter) were placed on straw mats and allowed to dry in the sun. These could be used in curries as required. The Banias also have a ceremony to mark the installation of the karaha, the area where the halwais are to prepare the wedding food. Utensils are honoured and some rock salt is ground. After the wedding the new son-in-law kicks away the temporary fireplace.

The daily cooking was usually done by the women of the household with the help of servants. I remember that in my grandfather's house there was a separate kitchen for vegetables, dal and roti, while the khansama presided over the main kitchen with a masalchi to do the donkey work. For special occasions, however, professional cooks were hired. The meat was made by bawarchis who brought their own helpers to do all the chopping and grinding. The boss only did the actual cooking. These bawarchis had their own special recipes which were zealously guarded and handed down from father to son. Halwais made the vegetables, mithai and savouries. At weddings, apart from the usual sweets, elaborate pakwans were made. These were large circles of dough, as much as a foot in diameter which were crimped and pricked and then fried golden, some kept plain and some sugared. After the wedding, pieces of pakwan along with sweets and savouries were given to the guests to take home.

In my family, picnics were occasions we all looked forward to. The extended family consisting of about twenty of us would set out armed with tiffin-carriers, surahis of water and the impedimenta for cooking as often the meat and pulao was cooked on the spot. I remember that my father's uncle, a portly gentleman who was a wonderful cook, would settle down in front of the angeethi the moment we arrived at our venue. The servants scurried around following his instructions and soon wonderful aromas would fill the air. Besides family-owned orchards, Humayun's Tomb, Qutub Minar and Okhla were favourite destinations. Food for travel was typically keema-matar, sookhe alu and poori. Snacks such as kachauri, mathri and besan ke ladoo were also carried as they do not spoil.

Delhi is known for a variety of snacks such as dahi ki gujiya (made with moong dal), kalmi bare (made with urad dal), papri chaat, alu-kachalu, fruit chaat and alu ke kulle. These are potatoes roasted in charcoal embers, peeled, hollowed and filled with a mixture of masalas and lemon juice. It is said that if you have not heard of Sultan ke kulle you are not a true Dilliwala—Sultan being the gentleman famous for the best kulle in town.

There are many mithais typical to Delhi such as piste ki lauz, made with coarsely crushed pistachios and sugar, badam ki lauz similarly made using almonds, kesar paag using desiccated coconut, sugar and saffron, imarti, elaborate loops of urad-dal paste fried and soaked in sugar syrup—a posh cousin of jalebi, which of course is a perennial favourite. Some vegetables such as petha and parval are steeped in sugar syrup to make mithai; the latter being deseeded and filled with khoya and nuts. Milk sweets include halva sohn and habshi halva, so called because khoya, sugar and ghee are cooked till deep brown and chewy. Then there is khurchan which literally means scrapings; it is made by heating milk in a large, shallow pan, skimming the skin that forms and sticking it against the sides of the pan. This is then scraped off and layered with sugar and rose water. Not having a long shelf life, it is usually made in winter. Rabri is another milk dessert that must be eaten fresh—if one arrives at the rabri and khurchan shops late in the afternoon chances are these sweets will have finished. Kheer is most commonly made by boiling milk with rice but sevian (vermicelli), ghia, carrots and lotus seeds are also used. Very finely ground rice and milk are cooked together to produce the delicately flavoured phirni. A particular favourite of my family was daulat ki chaat which is basically just sweetened milk foam. Traditionally chilled milk and cream-of-tartar was churned together and the resultant foam collected and layered with sugar and pistachios. Before the advent of refrigerators the milk was left outdoors and the overnight dew was supposed to be essential for the success of the recipe. I have followed my mother's recipe and made daulat-ki-chaat quite successfully with refrigerated milk using an electric whisk, though even then it takes hours to collect the foam. It is best eaten before the foam subsides. Another favourite is the kulfi, which dates back to Mughal times. In those days ice was brought to Delhi from the mountains in the north, the closest of which was the perennially snow-capped Choori Chandni ka Dhar near Kasauli. Then, as now, thickened milk, sweetened with sugar was poured into earthen moulds, sealed with dough and immersed in a mixture of ice and saltpeter, and shaken gently till frozen. Kulfi made in metallic moulds and served on a plate is now available but nothing matches the flavour of kulfi eaten on a bamboo stick from an earthen mould. Fortunately there are still people who make and bring a 'baraf-ki-handi' to weddings and parties. According to a Mathur custom, when a bride went to stay with her parents (in the same city), her in-laws would send a baraf-ki-handi and a khomcha of chaat (the chaat vendor with his paraphernalia) to demonstrate their affection for the new bride. There were also various halwas made with sooji, dal, ghia, kaddu, bajra and carrot—all oozing ghee and rich with nuts.

Many communities in Delhi were and are vegetarian. The Banias and Jains even eschewed onions and garlic and this has continued to the present day. Food is cooked in ghee or mustard oil and flavoured with spices including methi-dana (fenugreek seeds) and hing (asafoetida). Spinach and beetroot are often added to dough to make colourful poories.

Festivals are a time for eating and particular foods are associated with certain festivals. At Eid it is sevian which can be cooked with milk to make kheer, and with ghee added to make the rich muzafar and sheer khurma. During Ramzan the bazaars around the Jama Masjid are a gourmet's delight with mountains of biryani, kebabs of every kind, qorma and curries, rotis and naans, huge earthen pots of kulfi nestling in crushed ice, water ices, phirni, fragrant halwas, and little almond biscuits being freshly made on a tava. The festival of Sankrant is in January when til (sesame) and gur (jaggery) laddus are made which are supposed to ward off the cold. The Teej festival during the monsoon is associated with andarse ki goli (sweet ground-rice balls, coated in sesame and fried); sugared vermicelli is made at Raksha Bandhan. At Holi when the chickpeas are green one has boont ke laddu and sweetened khoya and nut-filled gujiyas. Gujiyas are also made at Diwali. For these two festivals a savoury papri is also made. Unlike the small flour papris used in chaat, these are made with spiced besan dough which is thinly rolled into large circles and fried till it is golden. Lotus seed kheer, sugared nuts, lotus seeds and melon seeds are usually given to new mothers and therefore made at Janamashtmi, a festival celebrating birth. In Khatri households at Janamashtmi, a tiny image of Lord Krishna tied with a silken thread is placed inside a hollowed cucumber. At midnight the thread is gently pulled and Krishna is 'born', bathed in milk and placed in a cradle.

Given the wide variety of food on offer, what was typical Delhi food? Allowing for differences in religion, community and class, the Dilliwalla traditionally had two main meals—a substantial morning meal which could be nahari kulcha or bedvin (a pitthi-stuffed poori) with alu and a saunf ki chutney and halwa, or nagauri (a small crisp semolina poori) with halwa and alu kachori before going to work. (Nagauri eaten with bhunva kofta was prescribed as a cure for a cold by my husband's grandfather.) Plenty of snacks were available during the day, and most people had an early dinner.

The menu obviously differed from one community to the next, but in all cases it was a fairly heavy meal. This routine is still prevalent among many families, especially among the trading community.

With the coming of the British and the nine-to-five office hours, the old system was replaced by the breakfast-lunch-tea-dinner regime. Indians working for the British had perforce to change their food habits; many affluent Indians adopted western lifestyles and food habits with bacon and eggs for breakfast and western food at dinner. Indian influences too worked on British dietary habits and the Raj cuisine was born. Initially this mélange of British and Indian cooking developed in south India and Calcutta and dishes like mulligatawny soup (from the Tamil word for pepper-water) were created. When the British made Delhi their capital this mixed heritage became a feature of Delhi food. Innovative Indian cooks learnt to tenderize goat meat to make it more palatable for the memsahibs. Using garlic and ginger to marinate meat gave a decidedly Indian flavour to roast mutton, chicken and pork. Meat from the ribs was beaten thin, marinated, crumbed and fried to produce mutton 'chaaps'; mince was used to make cutlets, rissoles, shepherd's pie and scotch eggs. (No one really knows whether the scotch egg came first or the nargisi kofta.) The Indian khichri became 'kedgeree' by substituting dal with smoked fish and hard-boiled eggs and was had for breakfast. The curry and rice produced by the khansamas was a mongrel mixture of vegetables, including bhindi, cooked with meat and spices and was truly awful! Amazingly Indian cooks learnt to bake delicious cakes, pies and biscuits with nothing more than a simple 'bake-pan', a circular pan around six inches deep with a tight-fitting lid. This was put on an open coal fire and the temperature was judged by hand. Desserts included baked custard, bread pudding, fruit trifle and crème caramel, known all over India as caramel custard. This is also referred to as 'dak bungalow pudding'!

Delhi expanded rapidly after 1947 with more and more people from all over India coming to live and work here and a vast variety of regional and international foods soon became available. The Punjabis were the first to add to the rich culinary heritage of Delhi. The famous Moti Mahal started by the charismatic Kundan Lal popularized tandoori food, particularly chicken. It is said that at his request Pandit Jawaharlal Nehru was served tandoori chicken from Moti Mahal on flights. The ubiquitous butter chicken was also a Moti Mahal creation. I remember going to the restaurant with my father and Kundan Lal had a waiter bring us a dish which he said was an innovation only tried the previous day. That was my first taste of the now famous butter chicken. I claim butter chicken as a Delhi dish as it was invented here. Even Karim's, the restaurant for 'original' Delhi food, has added it to their menu. 'Ishtoo', now a speciality of every Muslim restaurant, has transformed the bland English stew into a truly Indian dish.

In Delhi there are countless restaurants offering Mughlai food—mutton and chicken cooked in gravies full of tomatoes or thickened with cashew nuts and enriched with cream and butter, also 'Shahjahani raan' and 'shahi murg'. For vegetarians the term 'shahi' is added to paneer, alu or any other vegetable. All these bear very little resemblance to what the Mughals actually ate. But, as I said earlier, cookery is an ever-evolving art with new and exciting recipes being concocted all the time. The cuisine of Delhi, like the city itself, has adapted and adopted the dishes and ingredients from the many peoples and communities who have settled here and made it their home.

Dal Ki Kaleji (Green Bean Cubes in Gravy)

Serves 6 to 8

Traditionally the Mathurs have made vegetarian dishes look like meat. For dal ki kaleji, husked green beans are soaked and ground to a paste. This is boiled, cut into cubes, fried and cooked in a gravy to resemble liver though it does not taste in the least like liver!

Kaleji:

200 gm (one cup) husked green beans (dhuli mung ki dal)
2 medium onions, quartered
2 green chilies, deseeded and finely chopped
½ inch piece ginger, finely chopped
2 tsp fresh coriander, chopped
½ tsp salt
¼ tsp baking soda
250 gm (1¼ cups) ghee for frying

Gravy:

100 gm (½ cup) ghee
4 medium onions, ground
10 cloves garlic, ground
1 inch piece ginger, ground
3 tsp coriander seeds, powdered
½ tsp turmeric powder
2-3 tomatoes, skinned and chopped
4 tbsp curd
1 tsp salt
½ tsp garam masala powder
1 tbsp fresh coriander, chopped

Kaleji: Wash dal and soak for 8–10 hours in water. Drain and grind to a fine paste along with onions. Mix in the remaining ingredients and beat thoroughly. Put into a clean piece of muslin or napkin, and tie securely.

Have a large pan of boiling water ready and put in tied up dal. Boil for one minute, then reduce heat and simmer for 45 minutes. Lift out and cool slightly. Unwrap cooked dal and cut into ½-¾ inch cubes.

Heat 250 gms ghee in a kadhai or deep frying pan and fry cubes till golden. Drain and keep aside.

Gravy: Heat 100 gm ghee and fry ground onions golden. Add garlic and ginger and fry for two minutes, adding 1–2 tsp water. Stir in coriander powder, turmeric and tomatoes and cook for 5–7 minutes till mixture is paste-like. Add whipped curd, salt, garam masala and fresh coriander, pour in 500 ml water and simmer for 5 minutes. Put in pieces of fried dal, cover and cook on low heat for 10 minutes.

Ravi Dayal

A Kayastha's View of Delhi

Delhi is vast, and it is said to be a microcosm of India; it is inhabited liberally by people from all parts of the country and shared by all. Apart possibly from the politicians who infest the city and have appropriated the prettiest real estate in it for themselves, do people still think of themselves as Dilliwallahs, as the Mathur Kayasthas of Delhi once did?

Born of Mathur parents, and having had an association with Delhi for as long as I can remember (i.e. from circa 1940), I have periodically thought of myself as an authentic Dilliwallah. Although much of my childhood was spent outside Delhi, we were annual winter migrants to the city over sixteen years when I joined Delhi University and where I stewed for the next five (1954–59). Thereafter, I was based outside Delhi for the next eleven years as a student and then a publisher, and have been a publisher here since 1971. My genes, college days and profession have conspired to tie me to the city and coloured my view of it, so in this brief piece I will restrict myself to what flows from these three elements.

One of the traditional conceits of the Mathurs of Delhi is that they consider themselves the highest form of a high species—perhaps less flamboyant than the Mathurs once based in Lahore, but infinitely more refined as speakers of a tongue untainted by Punjabi; a cut above those in Rajasthan, who servilely served provincial rulers and said *hukum*; somewhat similar to members of the community in Agra and Lucknow, but free of the small-town smugness of urban Uttar Pradesh. The Mathurs of Delhi also considered themselves Dilliwallahs par excellence, forgetting that the city is now barely aware of them.

My father's family was originally from Peepalmandi in Agra, but with innumerable relations in Delhi; my mother's family was once based in Chelpuri and Chiraykhana in the Old City—always referred to as *shahar* by insiders, and never as Shahjahanabad. Early in the twentieth century some Mathurs from these *mohallas* colonized spacious houses with large gardens in the Civil Lines area, mostly a swathe of land with ber orchards enclosed by Commissioner's Lane and Usmanpur (now Jumna) Road. Many of them were lawyers, some became civil servants, others taught Urdu and Persian in colleges, and some concentrated on enjoying good food and music. Qudsia Bagh and the Yamuna across Bela (now Ring) Road were abiding factors in their lives—the river kept the area fragrant and comparatively cool, its sandy banks yielding walks and melons.

Some Mathur families were persuaded by the early developers of New Delhi to move to the new city. They clustered around Connaught Place, on Barakhamba and Curzon (now Kasturba Gandhi) Roads, and areas like Babur Road and Hanuman Road. All retained strong connections with their kin in 'shahar' and the Civil Lines, and all the major shopping—whether for clothes, jewellery, spices, paan, tin boxes, books and stationery—was still done in the Old City.

You couldn't bypass shahar. The entry into Delhi was always by train, at the Old Delhi railway station (the New Delhi station was largely ceremonial until the 1950s). There were usually prolonged unscheduled halts of the train at the Ghaziabad and Shahdara railway stations and, invariably, on the old iron bridge spanning the Yamuna, from where passengers had the classical view of the dhobis of Delhi washing and drying clothes on the river bank. The last phase of the journey was exhilarating as the train chugged through the Salimgarh fort and skirted the walls of the Lal Qila: the sense of entering a great and historic city was palpable.

The journey to a home in very central New Delhi was done in a tonga or two, with tin trunks and holdalls and baskets piled high. The route was well-trodden, the streets the tonga clattered through celebrated: it went past the Public (now Har Dayal) Library, down Nai Sarak, then Chawri Bazar, past Qazi Hauz and on to Ajmeri Gate (through which the tonga went, the horse's hooves echoing), past Delhi (now Zakir Husain) College and eventually down and up the Minto Bridge slope (where the tonga moved at the pace of a pedestrian and a gleaming Connaught Place came into view). Old Delhi was not only an essential and hallowed part of the route, but also the place where people indulged in sharp practices (with elegance), sharp talk and, generally, were city-slickers in a city they ardently believed to be the acme of creation.

As late as the 1950s the most trusted doctors in Delhi were located in Chandni Chowk or Daryaganj, and the great tailor was Mohammad Umar, who functioned in a lane not far from Atma Ram's, the best bookshop in Delhi, and in the Kashmiri Gate area. You didn't know good cuisine unless you had eaten in shahar, and of the four stylish hotels in Delhi, only the Imperial was in New Delhi: the rest—the Cecil, the Swiss and Maidens—were in the Civil Lines area. When a West Indies cricket team first toured India, it was housed at Maidens, which rocked with calypso rhythms for the likes of Walcott, Weekes, Gomez and George Headley.

And yes, people went to shahar to see and ride in trams, perhaps the ricketiest, slowest and oldest trams in the world, but the only ones in north India. Not even Lahore could boast of trams. Shahar remained the heart and soul of Delhi throughout my days in Delhi University. Our movements circumscribed by poor public transport (perhaps the only element of continuity in Delhi), the lack of personal scooters, motorcycles and cars, an outing from the campus usually led to Kashmiri Gate or the Jama Masjid area: we often walked there, and the route to Chandni Chowk meant using the high pedestrian bridge across the railway track near Kash Gate and often emerging from that exercise covered with soot from the puffing steam engines below as they pulled wagons to or from the Old Delhi station.

Until the late 1950s even those living outside the city walls knew shahar reasonably well. New and Old Delhi together still formed a comparatively compact unit, with New Delhiwallahs making regular forays into shahar and the Civil Lines areas: Moti Mahal was a premier attraction, and the bar and nightclub at Maidens the fanciest in town. The Ring Road hadn't yet come into being, so people couldn't ignore the Old City.

The journey to the university meant rides through Daryaganj and past Lal Qila, frequently involving prolonged halts in these areas as buses were changed. During these halts one got to know the *dhabas* and stalls near the bus stands, and, if a suitable bus failed to turn up, the journey was often continued on foot or temporarily abandoned in the *galis* of the Old City. Commuters thus got to know the bookshops in Daryaganj and Nai Sarak, and the *kabariwallas* near the Jama Masjid. These meanderings also prevented some of us from forgetting the Urdu script entirely, for the hoardings and signboards in the Old City were still mostly in Urdu and it was reassuring to be able to decipher them.

The cohesive, urbane combine of New and Old Delhi no longer exists and while Delhi has grown into a vast city over the last few decades, its different parts don't seem to make up a whole. The area covered by it appears to have reverted to what it was before shahar came into being—a collection of disconnected villages, each with its own ways and mannerisms, and altogether more provincial than the stylish, integrated city of not so long ago.

The village I inhabit, roughly extending from the Lodi Gardens to the Purana Qila, with Khan Market, several schools and Sujan Singh Park as its focal points, and the India

International Centre, India Habitat Centre, Humayun's Tomb, the Oberoi Hotel and Taj Mansingh at its periphery, is agreeable enough, but it's not a distinctive civilization, as Delhi once was. It is, nevertheless, a central area in a city that has expanded thirty kilometres afield in all the cardinal directions, and is visited by and known to people living in the outbacks. But most of the outbacks are less fortunate and remain strangers to each other.

There is, thus, no such thing as a Dilliwallah any more, and this absence seems to be part of the present, amorphous identity of the city. There are Londoners and New Yorkers, Parisians and Mumbaikars, Mysoreans and Hyderabadis, but the inhabitants of Delhi are now anonymous. Even the Mathurs have stopped calling themselves Dilliwallahs. How can it be otherwise if you live in GK II, your spouse perhaps a Sikh, your son an investment banker in New York, your daughter-in-law an Italian and your grandson unable to digest a decent, spiced kebab made of goat meat?

While the Dilliwallah may have gone into oblivion, the other Kayastha conceit—of being traditionally literate and literary and, generally, good pen-pushers—has prospered in the changed environment. The Mathurs were quick to take to the new educational system introduced by the British and soon entered professions that needed the skills so acquired. Pedigree Mathur that I am, I became part of a comparatively new form of pen pushing in 1961—publishing, and from my publishing peep-hole have not only witnessed and participated in the flowering of publishing in Delhi over the last few decades, but also been struck by the spectacular growth in Delhi's educational system and intellectual infrastructure which catalysed publishing.

India's educational system is much derided, no doubt with good reason, but the good should not be interred with the bones: one of the good things is that in the hurly-burly of the last five decades, as Delhi shed its old scales and didn't quite refashion itself as a cohesive whole, it also became India's premier educational centre and a magnet for the country in this area. If Delhi has more automobiles than Mumbai, Kolkata and Chennai put together, it also probably has more authors than in these cities put together, and produces books in a similarly excessive proportion.

This wasn't always so. Until the mid-1960s, Bombay was the major publishing centre in the country, with Calcutta and Madras not far behind. The best book printers and binders were in these cities, and even in 1971, when the OUP opened its office on Ansari Road, its bigger books were usually typeset there or in Pondicherry. With every major publishing house shifting base to Delhi around then or soon after, the skills needed to make a decent book rapidly developed in the region, and Delhi now leads the field both in printing and publishing.

Initially it was Ansari Road in Daryaganj that hosted the publishing renaissance, and manuscripts from Delhi University that nourished it; but matching the expansion of the city further south and the growth of author-yielding institutions in other parts of the city, publishing too is no longer concentrated along the rim of the Old City. Penguin is now in Panchsheel, OUP on Jaisingh Road, Permanent Black in Patparganj and Ravi Dayal in a back-room facing a garden and a pomegranate tree in Sujan Singh Park.

While the Delhi I knew and sometimes felt I belonged to has been obliterated, its new and, in many ways, much nastier incarnation has nevertheless nourished me enormously with the ideas its contemporary scholars, thinkers and writers have generated. A live but violent and corrupt Delhi is not a pleasurable creature to endure, but for a publisher in India, 'If on earth there is a place of bliss / It is this, it is this, it is this' crazy city.

Notes on Authors

KHUSHWANT SINGH is India's best-known writer and columnist, and Sobha Singh's most famous son. He has been founder-editor of *Yojana* and editor of the *Illustrated Weekly of India*, the *National Herald* and *Hindustan Times*.

He has also published the classic two-volume *History of the Sikhs* and several works of fiction—*Train to Pakistan, I Shall Not Hear The Nightingale, Delhi* and *The Company of Women*. He has written several non-fiction books on Delhi, nature and current affairs as well as a number of translated works including the *Japji Sahib* and *Celebrating the Best of Urdu Poetry*.

Khushwant Singh was a Member of Parliament from 1980 to 1986. He was awarded the Padma Bhushan in 1974 but returned the decoration in 1984 in protest against the storming of the Golden Temple by the Indian Army. In 2007, he was awarded the Padma Vibhushan, India's second highest civilian honour.

UPINDER SINGH is a professor in the Department of History of the University of Delhi. Specializing in the history of ancient India, she has written on various issues related to ancient and early medieval inscriptions, social and economic history, religious institutions and patronage, the history of archaeology, and the modern history of ancient monuments. She is the author of several books—*Kings, Brahmanas, and Temples in Orissa: An Epigraphic Study, AD 300–1147* (Munshiram Manoharlal, 1994); *The Discovery of Ancient India: Early Archaeologists and the Beginnings of Archaeology* (Permanent Black, 2004); *Ancient Delhi* (Oxford University Press, 1999; 2nd edition, 2006); a book for children,

Mysteries of the Past: Archaeological Sites in India (National Book Trust, 2002); and most recently, *A History of Ancient and Early Medieval India: From the Stone Age to the 12th century* (Pearson Longman, 2008). She has two edited volumes—*Delhi: Ancient History* (Social Science Press, 2006) and (co-edited with Nayanjot Lahiri) *Ancient India: New Research* (Oxford University Press, 2009).

WILLIAM DALRYMPLE was born in Scotland and brought up on the shores of the Firth of Forth. He wrote the highly acclaimed best-seller *In Xanadu* when he was twenty-two. Shortly after this he moved to Delhi, where has now lived on and off for the last twenty years. He is the author of *City of Djinns*, a most wonderful book illustrated by his wife Olivia, which won the Thomas Cook Travel Book Award and the Sunday Times Young British Writer of the Year Award. *White Mughals* won the Wolfson Prize for History 2003 and the Scottish Book of the Year Prize. His most recent book, *The Last Mughal*, was longlisted for the Samuel Johnson Prize and won the Vodafone Crossword Indian Book of the Year Prize and the Duff Cooper Memorial Prize. His new book, *Nine Lives: In Search of the Sacred in Modern India* was published in 2009.

SUNIL KUMAR was a graduate student at the University of Chicago and has a doctorate from Duke University. He is a professor at the History Department, University of Delhi, but currently teaches at the School of Oriental and African Studies, London University. He has written *The Present in Delhi's Past* (Three Essays Collective, 2008), *The Emergence of the Delhi Sultanate* (Permanent Black, 2007) and edited *Demolishing Myths or Mosques and Temples* (Three Essays Collective, 2008). Together with Kunal Chakrabarti, he edited *Our Pasts II: Social Science Text Book in History for Class VII*, (NCERT) and with Munis Faruqui, Richard M. Eaton, and David Gilmartin, edited *Expanding Frontiers in South Asian and World History* (2009) and a Special Issue of *Modern Asian Studies*.

PRADIP KRISHEN directed some well-known movies (*Massey Sahib, In Which Annie Gives It Those Ones* and *Electric Moon*) before he became a naturalist and ecological gardener. He is writing a book about the wild flowers of the Delhi Ridge, and planting up native plant gardens at Jodhpur, Nagaur and in the north-west Himalayas.

NARAYANI GUPTA taught history at Indraprastha College and at Jamia Millia Islamia, and is currently a consultant with INTACH. She was a founder member of the Conservation Society of Delhi (set up in 1984) and was advisor for *Delhi: The Built Heritage: a Listing* (INTACH 1999). She wrote *Delhi between Two Empires* (Oxford, 1981), updated Percival Spear's *Delhi: Its Monuments and History* (Oxford, 1997), co-edited *The Painter's Eye: Egron Lundgren and India* (National Museum, 1992), and co-authored *Beato's Delhi* (Ravi Dayal, 1997) and *Delhi Then and Now* (Roli Books, 2007).

VIDYA RAO who introduces the music of the Delhi gharana is not only a well-known thumri singer but also a scholar who has researched and written extensively on music. For many years, she was the disciple of Naina Devi and is currently receiving advanced training under Shanti Hiranand and Girija Devi. Her training in khayal gayaki has been under Professor B.N. Datta and Pandit Mani Prasad. She has composed and sung for the theatre and films and has been visiting professor at JNU's School of Arts and Aesthetics and Visiting Fellow at the Centre for Advanced Studies, Jadavpur University.

SOHAIL HASHMI is a genuine 'Dilliwalla'. He studied geography and regional development, and gave up academics to engage in unfashionable things like working in Delhi slums and with unorganized workers. He eventually drifted into the electronic media but had to start his own production house when every company he had joined folded up shortly after hiring him.

Between 2004 and 2008, Sohail was director of Leap Years, a creative activity centre for children. Currently, he is involved in conducting heritage walks, writing about lesser-known monuments of Delhi for *Landscape* magazine, and trying to start a foundation for documenting the heritage of Delhi. He writes scripts for documentaries and on the blogsite kafila.org. Sohail loves to eat and cook, and spends all his free time in the kitchen.

DUNU ROY is the Director, Hazards Centre, a unit of the Sanchal Foundation, assisting urban and rural communities in research and action programmes related to shelter, livelihoods, services, and governance, and in the struggle for justice by the urban poor. He is a chemical engineer by training and a consultant to multilateral and government agencies on resource management, environment, biodiversity and disaster preparedness in several states of India.

PRITI NARAIN belongs to an old family of Delhi and the Kayastha community which has a tradition of taking great pains over the preparation and serving of good food. She ran a gourmet restaurant in Delhi for two years, in partnership with a friend. For several years, she supplied cakes on order. Currently Priti leads a relaxed life, watching birds and taking the occasional order for chocolate cake.

RAVI DAYAL read history at St Stephen's and Oxford. He worked thereafter at the Oxford University Press for twenty-five years as chief editor and then its general manager. Under his stewardship, the OUP published the most distinguished Indian scholars in the social sciences—Salim Ali, Andre Beteille, Ranajit Guha, Irfan Habib, Ashis Nandi, A.K. Ramanujan, Amartya Sen, M.N. Srinivas and Romila Thapar.

In 1987, he set up his own publishing house, Ravi Dayal Publisher, which he ran entirely by himself, publishing primarily fiction, poetry and non-academic books. Included in his imprint were novelists like Amitav Ghosh and Mukul Kesavan, poets like Agha Shahid Ali, Keki Daruwalla and Arvind Krishna Mehrotra and dramatists like Girish Karnad. He also published excellent translations of some of the finest writers in the regional languages.

Ravi Dayal passed away in June 2006.

RAVI DAYAL [illegible] at St Stephen's and Oxford. He worked [illegible] Oxford University Press for [illegible] years [illegible] editor, and then [illegible] manager. [illegible] the OUP published the most [illegible] scholars [illegible] social sciences [illegible] [illegible] Ashis Nandy [illegible] [illegible]

In 198[illegible] he set up his own publishing house, Ravi Dayal Publisher, which he ran [illegible] publishing [illegible] [illegible] [illegible] [illegible] [illegible] [illegible] [illegible] writers in the country [illegible]

Ravi Dayal passed away [illegible] 2006.